To Sybil
Best Wishes
Sheila Ward

BEYOND WHITE MISCHIEF

BEYOND WHITE MISCHIEF

Memoirs of a Tea Planter's Wife

Sheila Ward

Book Guild Publishing
Sussex, England

First published in Great Britain in 2011 by
The Book Guild Ltd
Pavilion View
19 New Road
Brighton, BN1 1UF

Typesetting in Garamond by
Keyboard Services, Luton, Bedfordshire

Printed and bound in Great Britain by
CPI Antony Rowe

A catalogue record for this book is available from
The British Library

ISBN 978 1 84624 616 6

Contents

To my children

Growing Up

My earliest memories are of cretonne curtains, in blurry pale pastel shades. I used to chew them. I can still feel my teeth on edge thinking of it. We lived in a three-bedroom two-storey house in Oakfield Road, Gosforth, a suburb of Newcastle-on-Tyne. I was born in the local nursing home at midday on Wednesday 29th August 1932. I joined two other girls, Patricia (or Pat), three years older, and Agnes (or Nan), seven years older. My mother told me there had been a boy, four months in the womb, but my father kicked her in the stomach and she lost him. I don't know if this was true, but it doesn't sound the sort of thing you make up. She hated him with venom.

On the gate was the name 'Struan'. There was a modest lawn in front of the house, flowerbeds round the edge, and a delicate Japanese flowering cherry in the centre. Its pale-pink papery flowers reminded me of the artificial ones that open up in a glass of water, displaying the same pearly gradations of colour. Behind the house was a patio area with a comfortable swing/settee; its canvas smell, and the broad-striped green and yellow shadows join the curtains as early memories. Beyond that was a vegetable garden, carefully tended by my mother who was keen on fresh vegetables.

There was a three-legged oak stool, made by the Blind School. Upside down, it was my car, ship, horse, anything. I loved dolls, and Mummy sewed and knitted the most beautiful clothes for them. I had a golliwog, a teddy bear of course, and a much-loved rocking horse. Later on a Post Office set, with stamps, envelopes, rubber stamps, ink pads, became my favourite – very Virgoan. I was always a tidy child.

Winter in the north-east of England was very cold, wet and frequently snowy. We had to take a hot bath every morning followed by freezing cold squirts from the hand-held shower nozzle, 'to close the pores'. She didn't believe in warm scarves, no, it would 'coddle us'! It was the medical fashion in the 1930s to hold parties so that the children of the neighbourhood would all catch various childhood diseases. I caught measles, chicken pox, German measles, whooping cough, mumps, but I didn't catch scarlet fever. Pat got that and it was severe enough for her to be confined to the fever isolation hospital in the centre of the Town Moor.

In retrospect I feel that, certainly in my case, it was too much of a good thing, especially as all these happened one after another, with no time to really recuperate. I ended up with a weak chest. Dr Freeman was our tall, handsome GP, I was always glad to see him, a frequent visitor. Then I came down with appendicitis and suffered the indignity, at five years of age, of being wheeled around in a large pram afterwards. We met an Old English sheepdog and he poked his huge head into the pram – I thought he was a lion! The story goes that they found an open nappy pin in my appendix, a hard one to swallow. On the other hand it could have been my habit of chewing privet leaves from our hedge, pretending they were fillets of fish, or trying to cook potatoes over a candle flame ... and eating them raw.

When I got back from the hospital I found they had given away some of my favourite playthings to the orphanage, including my beloved rocking horse ... didn't they expect me back?

My mother was ahead of her time as far as healthy diet was concerned. Fresh fruit, raw salads, brown bread, restricted amounts of sweets (only after meals). Regular visits to the dentist kept our teeth in good order. She was a wonderful cook, made pies, cakes pastries, tarts ... she tried to teach me, but I was keen on the tasting part, licking the bowl, not beating up butter and sugar – 'creaming' – that was too much like hard work. The kitchen was large, with a square pine table where we had breakfast. There was a gas oven, overhead a pulley for airing clothes, and in the scullery a primitive washing machine with a mangle for wringing out the wet clothes.

We had maids, dailies, who wore red and white check gingham for ordinary work, and black dresses for special occasions, with a pin-on lace-edged apron and tiara-shaped cap. They didn't last long as a rule; mother was a tough mistress. They all seemed to have the same smell – sweat and furniture polish.

Sabina Espessiva was a refugee from the Spanish War of Independence. Shiny black hair pulled back in a bun, little scared black eyes, flash of gold in her teeth, smell of garlic, and above all, very little English.

One day she threw away my mother's teeth – a bridge that reposed in a glass of water beside the bed. What a screaming match! The teeth were found in the garbage of course, but oh the sight of my gap-toothed mother waving her arms about in a paroxysm of fury. Big loss of face. Poor Sabina, not long after that she ran away with a romantic Basque onion seller. The onion sellers used to come over on their bicycles with long strings of orange onions hanging down their shoulders, cigarette nonchalantly in one corner of the mouth, little beret tip-tilted to one side, and one gold earring. I like to think of Sabina and her beau cycling through the lanes of Brittany, with her perched on the crossbar in front of him.

Every Sunday we would have a large roast either leg of lamb, or round of beef, with Yorkshire pudding cooked in the pan with the beef, and roast potatoes, peas, brussels sprouts, gravy, then apple pie or sponge pudding, so we would have to go for a long boring walk, a 'constitutional' my father would call it. He'd stride ahead with his walking stick, he always used it, but nowadays very few men do – only elderly people. In those days he always wore a hat out of doors, a homburg usually. I would squeeze the tar bubbles in the fences as we walked by, or collect horse chestnuts if it was that time of year, to be dried and hung on a string for the game of conkers. I longed for a dog to take for walks. We did adopt a red setter at some stage, but the poor thing pined, it needed lots of space and our garden wasn't big enough so we had to give it away. But we always had cats, usually Persians.

My father, Peter, had a job selling things to do with engineering … and roads I think. He was from Stirling, where his father had a newsagent's shop in the main street. My father was going to study naval architecture at the university, but his strictly religious father, Andrew Ferguson, caught him 'drinking champagne out of an actress's slipper' or so the story goes. He threw him out of the house, and Peter ran away to sea, joined the Merchant Navy and went to the Far East where he picked up some bad habits, including a taste for whisky. I can't help thinking he must have done something far more immoral than that! Anyway his younger brother Andrew became the favoured son and garnered the benefits, such as going to university, and becoming a well-respected dental surgeon in Seaford.

The next refugee was Inge Baum, a large friendly young German Jewess who tried to teach me the basics of German. 'In das Haus der ist ein Maus' was as far as I remember. She didn't manage to teach me much else, and as the war came nearer perhaps my parents began to doubt that a knowledge of that language was so desirable, so she left as well. I was too young to wonder what had happened to her. When much later I went to school in Germany it might have helped me to absorb the lingo, and I picked it up quite quickly.

Pat, Nan and I used to go to Sunday school, but my parents never went to church. My father announced he was an atheist; mother said she was an agnostic and could pray anywhere, preferably on the top of a hill, but I never spotted her doing any praying anywhere let alone on top of a hill, she was too much of this world. Only later on when I had children of my own did I realise that it was the only real privacy they had – a 'lie-in' on a Sunday morning. Peter had had the kirk forced down his throat three times a day.

I started going to kindergarten at four and a half, dressed in a brown poplin smock, (which I also chewed). In winter we wore the ugliest brown knitted cap with ear flaps that you pulled down in the wind, brown mittens attached to tapes, thick brown stockings attached to my liberty bodice (the same as a suspender belt, but in a vest form – why 'liberty' I don't know, it was pretty restricting), combinations (thermal long johns like a man's with an opening between the legs for easy access), and wellies if it was raining. I was very proud of the fact that I could tie up my own shoelaces (with much sticking out of tongue). Dressing took forever! Pat and Nan rode off on two-wheeler bicycles and I followed them on my big tricycle, trying to catch up in the heavy traffic on the main road to town, battling with the trams and tram lines, let alone cars and lorries.

I was left-handed right from the start, even sucked my left thumb till I was five, Mummy tried to change it, in those days being left-handed was considered extremely bad form. At school they used to slap my hand when I used it, but a stubborn streak made me even more determined. On my first day at school I made clay bananas, painted them yellow, then went on to apples and pears. At break time I wandered round the asphalt playground, then squatted against the fence to eat biscuits out of my hinged tin box, 'fly' biscuits –

4

currants with a slightly burnt taste. My favourites were fig slices, or icing ones, with figures on them of what resembled dodos, but were meant to be swans, elephants, fairies, and which were in demand for swapping.

The next day I was shown how to make an African kraal: plasticine round-huts and matchstick fencing with stick figures. In the playground I soon found out that my 'lah-de-dah' accent made me an unpopular child. Mummy had never let me play with the 'common' children, with their shaven, ring-wormed heads and shoeless feet, although I dearly wanted to ... I don't know how she expected me to avoid them in school.

I learnt to read very quickly – it was a wonderful escape from the terrible rows that increased with each year, as my mother's nagging and my father's drinking escalated. I would read with a torch under the covers, and in any corner I could find, especially when there was washing-up, or silver cleaning to be done. Mummy would read to us in bed at night of course, fairy stories with incredibly delicate illustrations by Edmund Dulac or Arthur Rackham, or *The Arabian Nights*.

When Disney started producing his wonderful feature length cartoons we went to see them all: *Bambi, Dumbo, Snow White, Sleeping Beauty*. We also saw *The Wizard of Oz*. The illustrated stories had pictures of the wicked queen who turns into a witch, and I could never look at those pictures. I had nightmares after seeing the films. At night the coal fire would cast evil leaping shadows on the wall. One night there was a rare dinner party going on downstairs and I wanted to wee very badly but I was too terrified to get out of bed. I screamed myself hoarse but no one came. I thought a combination of Captain Hook, Charles II and the Wicked Witch of the West were under the bed! The next morning Mummy discovered I'd wet the bed and couldn't understand how I could do such a thing (at four and a half). It was the long black ringlets that really horrified me – connecting King and pirate!

Apart from the awful cold, I loved winter. We gathered round the fire and toasted teacakes, crumpets or muffins. Sometimes we roasted chestnuts in the embers. We'd have tea on the big brass tray Daddy had brought home from the East. On the mantelpiece three ebony elephants paraded in descending sizes, and we had many brass vases and ornaments that he'd collected. He also collected first editions, but those were carefully locked away in a cabinet.

When the first heavy snow fell we'd take our sledges to the Town Moor. There was a special hill where everyone went – some people only had tin trays, but all had a great time. We would have snowball fights, I specially loved them, the only time we could show any aggression to our domineering father and get away with it! Then building a snowman. Of course the downside was chilblains and slush in the road. I believed in Father Christmas until I was about seven, when Nan poured scorn on me for still believing in him.

We used to go to parties in beautiful velvet cloaks of emerald, sapphire and crimson, with swansdown collars, made by Mummy, of course. She was a very good seamstress and made most of our clothes. Thanks to her skills we were always well turned out, even when our income was low, although she never worked – it just wasn't done in those days. On special occasions we would wear our tartan kilts and tweed jackets.

Once she was in the middle of sewing a pale-green pure silk dress for my birthday; it had only one frill at the neck and at the hem, and I thought it rather plain. She had to go to hospital for some mysterious 'woman's ailment' (we were always kept in the dark about such things), and I was whining that she wouldn't finish it in time for my party. Her best friend, Elsie Coulson, turned to me and snapped, 'How can you be so selfish? Your mother is going into hospital and you bother her about a thing like that. How selfish you are!'

I was so ashamed, I loved my mother dearly, and I never forgot that remark. She was back in one piece two days later, and finished the dress in time.

One day I went to see a friend who lived in the big house opposite us. She had a cold and couldn't come out to play. Dawdling down the drive I spotted her new doll's pram. It was forest green, cream inside, and was specially made for twin dolls. The two identical dolls wore silken lace-edged dresses, and matching underwear and bootees, and they had lovely curly blonde hair. How could her family leave these two out in the drive, it might rain! Holding onto the handle I thought, Why not take them for a little walk? Just down to the end of the road.

The glory of it intoxicated me. Passers-by stopped to admire the stately pram and its occupants. I invented names for them, and a whole history. Soon I realised I was a long way from home, so I might as well carry on. On the Town Moor the full-moon-shaped street lights were switching on, and I began to feel uneasy. A thin woman in a black leather raincoat, with Eton-cropped hair and smoking a cigarette, was coming towards me. She asked me in a broad Geordie accent, 'Whear you goin', hinny?'

I just stared at this apparition.

'Why don' you come hoam wi me? I'll gie you sweeties!' she asked.

Even I knew it was bad manners to smoke in the street. She looked weird, and she spoke in the way my mother hated. Also Mummy had always dinned into me never to take sweets from strangers. Suddenly I realised – she was a witch, and if I went with her she would lure me into her gingerbread cottage and eat me! The poor woman probably meant to hand me over at the nearest police station, but panic overwhelmed me and next thing I was flying helter-skelter back the way I'd come. The dolls began to fall out of the pram and I had to swipe them up as I racketed towards the traffic lights of the main road.

Once over the road I stopped. It was dusk and everything looked different, how was I to get home? An elderly man who looked vaguely like Father Christmas told me how to find Oakfield Road. Happily I arrived at my house, to find an angry reception committee. Instead of being glad and relieved to see me after my epic adventure, they were shouting furiously, and Daddy gave me the most agonising beating on my bare bottom. What would people think, stealing my friend's doll's pram? It was no use protesting that I only meant to take the pram for a little walk, they didn't want to know. At the big house they took the pram back with raised eyebrows, and I never played with that friend again.

I never forgave my father for that beating. My parents always said they didn't believe in corporal punishment, but his brutal treatment of my mother, and now myself, formed a core of resentment against him, and against men, that would influence the rest of my life.

Pat and I shared a wonderful rapport, and she was a great comfort after the pram debacle. Each night in bed we became Mrs Black and Mrs Brown, swapping gossip over the garden fence, using different characters and accents, incorporating daily events. Later, when radio acting became the mainstay of my career, I would think back to those nights, and realise that all the practice imitating strange accents had paid off.

My father decided to teach me to ride a two-wheeler bicycle. As usual I was a complete duffer with no sense of balance. He wanted me to be the boy he never had, but I was a woeful weakling. Still, in the end I mastered it, after crashing into the wall of the cul-de-sac at the end of our road a few times. Roller skating on steel skates that could be unscrewed and lengthened as one's feet got bigger, was the next big craze. Then there was no stopping me!

Some weekends in the summer we would go to St Mary's Isle in the Wolseley. I loved the leather seats and stylish walnut dashboard – a really solid family car. Our neat wicker basket had everything attached by straps to the sides. Picnics were laid out on a tartan rug, then a snowy tablecloth, tea made with the dainty spirit kettle, pre-cut cucumber or liver paste sandwiches, everything tasting vaguely of meths. Rushing down to the beach, we would bury each other in the sand, or carve out boats and castles. My father tried to teach me to swim, by chucking me into the surf. I, of course, disappointed him by promptly drowning – or starting to! We loved walking along the pier to the lighthouse, watching the sea boil and crash below the green pebble-glass lozenges under our feet.

Instead of the beach we often went into the marvellous Northumbrian countryside, to find a wood carpeted with bluebells, have a picnic, then go looking for mushrooms in nearby fields, or gathering blackberries in the hedgerows. We followed the old Hadrian's Wall that stretches right across to the west, imagining Roman cohorts marching along there, looking out for Picts and Scots.

My father was a very keen golfer, with a seven handicap. His father used to encourage him to play from an early age, on the slopes of Stirling castle. He was also a member of the Newcastle Aero Club, and we'd go there to watch him flying. He made beautiful model aeroplanes and also a model of the *Golden Hind*, Drake's ship. He was a Mason, and once I was looking for clothes to dress up in and found a leather pouch with his regalia – softest kid apron with dazzling stalactites resembling Christmas decorations and purple ribbon rosettes. Mummy caught me and was very shocked; she said it was a secret.

He was very neat, and always wore highly polished shoes, kept in shoe-trees in the wardrobe. He had neatly folded shirts, their separate collars arranged together artistically in rows His fingernails were immaculate; sometimes he would catch me at night and put me on his knee and start to cut my nails, pushing down the quicks with a kind of contained ferocity. When in a good mood he would sing 'Bumpety, bumpety, bumpety bump, here comes the galloping Major', swinging me energetically on his knee, or 'This is the way the lady rides...', a gentle trot, or 'This is the way the farmer goes, hobbledehoy, hobbledehoy', very jerky. Then a final bump and he'd drop me on the floor. I loved these times, which were few and far between. Kissing me goodnight I would smell the whisky on his breath, I've never been able to drink whisky because of that memory.

He loved the 'Skye boat song' about Bonnie Prince Charlie and Flora McDonald, and all the old Scottish songs, 'The road to the isles', 'Annie Laurie', 'Loch Lomond'. We would sing these songs as we drove up to Stirling once a year to stay with the grandparents, then we'd start on 'The old grey mare she ain't what she used to be', 'Ten green bottles', and 'Pop goes the weasel' (which refers to pawning something), and play 'I Spy' endlessly. I, of course, was frequently car-sick, and Mummy would flourish a handkerchief soaked in eau-de-cologne, so of course now whenever I smell it I feel sick!

The first person to spot the Wallace Monument looming over the pine trees in the distance would earn a sixpence – that's how I found out I was short-sighted, because I never saw it first. Then I had to have glasses, but I never wore them until much later: too vain, and afraid of ridicule.

Granpa was a tallish, slim man with crisp, curly brown hair, twinkling blue-green eyes, and a mock-stern manner. As well as running his newsagent's shop, he was a well-known antiquarian with a keen interest in Stirling history. He supplied a number of articles and wrote numerous letters to the paper. When courting my grandmother

Mummy in Dalry, Scotland   Daddy   Uncle Arthur

Mummy   Left to right: Pat, Peter, Andrew, Nan and
Sheila in Stirling

Mother's Aunt Kate and
Uncle Edwin Tower

he showed a surprisingly romantic side, writing poetry, drawing sketches of her, singing and playing his violin to her. Agnes Crerar Macnab was a tall blonde girl with a serene manner. But by the time we knew her she had become rather fat, always wore long black dresses, and smelled of 'baps'. These were the delicious floury-coated rolls that she baked for breakfast every morning.

'Come ben an I'll mash the tay,' (come in and I'll make tea), was her typical greeting to us after our long trek from Newcastle.

They lived in a double-storey house with four bedrooms, a small garden in front with rose bushes under the windows, a pebbled path leading from the gate. The crunch of dry pebbles underfoot reminds me of Stirling. The house smelled of baps, Pears soap, apples and a faint undercurrent of urine from the big chamber pots under the feather beds. Jugs and ewers decorated with roses were in each bedroom, but there was a bathroom with an old-fashioned claw-footed bath, and a wooden-topped loo. Granpa's razor strop hung beside the mirror, his cut-throat razor and brush on a shelf.

There were some quite valuable paintings in the hall and sitting room, of Bonnie Prince Charlie (naturally), Mary, Queen of Scots, and various dark-brown paintings of Ferguson, Macnab and Robertson ancestors. On the mantelpiece were more elephants from my father's travels.

The back garden was our favourite place: large, dotted with fruit trees, a big vegetable patch, and right at the end a beautiful little burn, sparklingly clear, where we fished for 'minnies' (minnows) with nets and jam jars. Other children from the nearby gardens would join us, especially Nancy Plank with whom we had a kind of love-hate relationship. 'Bloody Sassenachs,' was her usual greeting!

Sometimes we'd go to Macarthur's Park to play on the swings. A band of local children would gather and shout insults, I never liked the park, it had thick, dark pine trees louring over the swings, there was something malign about that place. Nan sat on a hornets' nest once and was badly stung, so we stopped going there.

Sundays were purgatory, traipsing back and forth to the kirk in our wee kilts. Granpa gave us huge peppermints to stay off the pangs of hunger and boredom. No wonder my father was atheistic. The outings to Stirling Castle and to Edinburgh were highlights of our stay, and we had miniature golf clubs to play with on the castle slopes. Daddy was in the Argyll and Sutherland Highlanders as a youth, and played the pipes, but his main regret was that he was too young to fight in the First World War (I would have thought he was very lucky, since his chances of remaining alive would have been quite slim).

Aunt Mary and Uncle Jimmy Macnab lived in nearby Cecil Street. She wore curlers in her hair, ate chocolates and read trashy novels, whenever I saw her. They had no children.

We loved it when our cousins, Andrew and Peter Ferguson, came up to Stirling from Seaford. Peter and I were very much alike, fair-haired and blue-eyed, but Andrew had olive skin and brown eyes from his mother, Louey. I always had a slight crush on Peter. We developed a taste for weird things like haggis, kippers, tripe, and finnan haddie (haddock poached in milk), and always had porridge for breakfast in the winter. My father would eat it with salt and no milk. The sound of the bagpipes would fill me with patriotic fervour, and we all learned Scottish dancing. So when the false war started we were dismayed to hear there would be no more trips to Scotland, because of petrol rationing.

Up to the start of the war life was not very different from the beginning of the century. Tinkers wandered the streets calling out for pots and pans to mend, gypsies came to the door selling heather and hand-made wooden clothes pegs and offering to tell your fortune if you 'crossed her palm with silver'. My mother gave them short shrift: 'superstitious nonsense!' Rag and bone men sauntered along with their smelly cargo, the cart pulled by a droopy old nag, like Steptoe and Son. 'Gentlemen of the Road', old men with long silver beards and hair, came to the back door and would be given bread and butter and a mug of sweet tea.

There was no TV to fill up the hours, our parents listened to the wireless and played bridge with their friends, which of course meant more rows after the game when they had the postmortems. Children listened to radio series, *Toytown*, *Alice in Wonderland*, and later on *The Three Musketeers*. The signature tune was a snatch of music from the Suite Arlesienne, and for years I tried to find out where it came from. *Swallows and Amazons*, a series by Arthur Ransome about the Lake District, was a firm favourite.

At birthday parties we played spin the trencher (a round wooden bread board), postman's knock, grandmother's footsteps, hide and seek, pass the parcel. We danced round to 'Ring a ring a roses' (which remembers the Great Plague) saying 'Atishoo, atishoo all fall down', which indicates that someone died after sneezing, the first sign of the disease. Another rhyme was 'Ride a cock horse to Banbury Cross, to see a fine lady on a white horse', describing one of Elizabeth the First's progresses through the shires of England. She impoverished many squires by billeting herself and her considerable retinue on them! 'London Bridge is falling down' described the Great Fire of London of 1666. 'The Grand Old Duke of York, he had ten thousand men, he marched them up to the top of the hill, then he marched them down again' satirises an unfortunate incident in, I think, the Franco-Prussian War. It would be danced by two lines of children peeling off and joining up at the top.

We played draughts, snakes and ladders, noughts and crosses, and simple card games like snap and rummy. We weren't allowed to read comics, but we smuggled them in: Beano, Magnet, Boy's Own Paper. Outside I would play hopscotch, chalking it on the pavement, or marbles, or go down to the shops with my weekly pocket money (sixpence), to buy a pennyworth of acid drops, or strings of bootlace liquorish, or large black sweets which changed colour as you sucked them. Ices were usually frozen sweetened juice in triangular paper cones, a strange sensation as you bit the little pyramid of ice.

Near Christmas time was the most exciting event of the year: pantomime! I loved the fire curtain at the Theatre Royal. It had advertisements from the so-called Naughty Nineties, Gibson Girls with huge hats and tiny waists, can-can girls with long legs whirling out of frothing lace petticoats, adverts for beer, cigarettes etc. When it went up it revealed another curtain, red velvet with gold tassels. The orchestra tuned up in the pit, the lights went down, the curtains swept open, and onto the stage strode a boy (who was a girl) and an old woman (who was a man) ... that was the formula, whether you saw *Aladdin, Al Baba, Dick Whittington, Jack and the Beanstalk*, whatever. Strange that we accepted it without question, long before transvestites emerged publicly. I adored Pat Kirkwood, gorgeous legs, vivacious, and wanted to be her ... or at least, to be on that glittering stage, in a dream world. I didn't know how, but somewhere inside me the resolve grew.

My mother took us to classical concerts in the City Hall, mostly of romantic and popular composers, like Tchaikovsky, Rimsky-Korsakov, and Elgar, but my father seldom went with us: he called modernistic violin music 'bellyache music'. He liked the Music Hall, with vulgar comedians. He would laugh until he cried at someone like Max Miller. Mummy hated me to go with him, but as the jokes were above my head it didn't really matter – I just liked anything that pertained to the stage.

A Sunday treat was a visit to the docks. We watched skinny Lascars shinning up the rigging, and Daddy explained what life on a merchant ship was like. Once a fat hideously tattooed man writhed out of a huge arrangement of glistening chains – that gave me nightmares!

My mother still went to garden parties in lovely long georgette and chiffon dresses (which she made herself) and big picture hats. We still had a servant. Mummy still gave elegant little tea parties with cucumber sandwiches, thin bone china cups and saucers, a silver teapot on a silver salver. Morning coffee at Carricks, where the fashionable Jewish ladies held sway, awash with furs and jewellery, while a three-piece orchestra played tinkly music up in a gallery. Shopping at Fenwicks and Bainbridges with Elsie.

Meanwhile something was happening in Europe that we tried hard to ignore. Hitler was jack-booting it, Mussolini jutting his chin, Edward VIII had abdicated, but we just loved the replacement family anyway. We copied the style of the little princesses' clothes, and collected pictures of famous film stars and of the Canadian Dionne quins.

The War Years

Chamberlain went to Munich, and came back to announce 'Peace in our Time!' The Nazis marched into Poland. We declared war. An unnatural calm ensued, there were rumours that we would have to be evacuated when the bombing started. Schools were issued with gas masks. All windows had to have blackout curtains drawn at night. People started digging air raid shelters at the bottom of the garden.

We moved to Sunderland, and invested in a Morrison shelter – a large reinforced steel table with removable sides, inside which you could squeeze our family of five if necessary. Daddy got a job with Joblings, the glass factory. They made Pyrex dishes, and also top-secret glass instruments for submarines, which meant he was in a protected job and couldn't be called up.

When the bombing of industrial and shipping areas really started, the big evacuation scare began. We three sisters were sent to Keswick in Cumberland. We were billeted on a Miss Blackbeard. She had black hair, a visible moustache, and a black soul ... or so we thought, because she treated us as skivvies. We had to clean up after the lodgers and empty their foul-smelling chamber pots into the outdoor privy. This was reached by struggling down a narrow lane past overhanging tendrils of brambles, which grabbed at us as we squeezed by. Nettles stung our bare ankles, and the privy itself stank. Cut-up newspapers threaded onto string hung from a nail. On top of that the food was awful, and not much of it. Word reached my mother and she began to harass the authorities, so that we were sent to the Bellas's mixed dairy farm on the outskirts of Keswick.

What a contrast! The family and the farm labourers ate together in the big kitchen – huge rabbit pies, meat of all kinds from their own produce, home-churned butter, cream, free-run eggs, honey, apple pies, all dispensed happily with humour (no rationing there). I shared a little dormer-windowed bedroom with Pat, and we could look out over the orchard of crab apple trees. There was an inside loo as well!

I learned to look for the eggs, and generally helped around the

15

farm, made stooks at the hay-making and in fact was found asleep by Nan inside one after a long hard day. I was given a little Scotty dog of my own, which I took for walks every day. On one of these walks I met a War Correspondent, Mr Ward-Price, who lived with his sister in a cottage nearby. They both had wild curly grey hair and were very nice, they used to give me peppermints. We wrote each other letters, and he would draw strange animals and ask me to identify them. One was an armadillo, which stumped me. His peculiar brand of humour was a delight, and I wished my father was like him, but I suppose it was easy for a bachelor to enjoy the company of a child when it wasn't mandatory!

When school started, we caught a bus every day. I saw a friend from Newcastle and joined her queue to enrol with her class. No one seemed to realise that she was about two years older than me. I managed with most subjects, but my missing link regarding arithmetic meant I was mystified from the start. After a while the powers-that-be decided evacuation wasn't such a marvellous idea and we were returned to our parents. Strange, because by then the bombing had intensified.

Mummy was living in a rented cottage in Seahouses, a little fishing village not far from Bamburgh. Daddy was still in Sunderland, at Joblings. I don't know if their separation was voluntary, but we all enjoyed the lack of strife on the home front. He would spend occasional weekends with us, but seemed to be less aggressive. I suspect it was around this time that he formed an association with a Mrs Brown, a hard-faced, chain-smoking Geordie wife, whose children we detested. Next door was the Dunes Residential Hotel, and we started played ping-pong there with some children, but they were much older than I. So I became a solitary soul, wandering along the rock pools at low tide, discovering an aquatic world of infinite fascination.

Troops began to tunnel dug-outs in the dunes opposite the cottage. My mother and various helpers made huge tin jugs of sweet milky tea, which we would carry out to the soldiers. The dug-outs were decorated with cut-out pictures of Betty Grable, June Havoc, and any girl showing long bare legs.

There was a mine on the beach – round, with prongs sticking out all over it, just like a cartoon. I went up to it but didn't touch it. The demolition men came and detonated it. A cruiser blew up on the horizon, and racehorses, silk stockings, Hershey bars, all kinds of sodden cargo floated ashore. The racehorses were dead, horribly maimed. We went to the local flea-pit to watch news reels about the war, and saw how London was battered night after night in the Blitzkrieg and the little ships rescuing our soldiers from the Dunkirk beachhead. We'd walk home eating fish and chips wrapped in copies of the *News of the World*, recovering from the cigarette smoke in the cinema, watching the innocent-looking sea sparkling in the moonlight, our imaginations picturing U-boats lurking out there.

The fishermen went grimly on, they had no protection except faith. Once the catch was in the harbour, their bare-breasted wives would sit gutting the fish, yellow oilskins wrapped about their ample hips. Toni sold ice cream, but Toni was Italian and people were muttering that he should be interned We just wanted him to stay, he was a charming man with his black curly locks and white-toothed smile – and his ice cream was the best!

It was decided I would study with the two children of a family near Bamburgh Castle. Their governess was Miss Mather. She wore her hair in big beige sausage curls that would start to unwind in the sea air as the day went on. She was mad about Grace Darling, the local fisher girl who rowed out and rescued a whole lot of people from a shipwreck one night, and died. We'd have lessons, then go out to feed the hens with great buckets of smelly swill.

I loved the walk to and from Seahouses every day. Alongside the tarmac was a kind of swampy area, velvety and warm under bare feet, all kinds of wild flowers, purple vetch, yellow colt's foot, cushiony grasses, sometimes snails. On the other side were the dunes, with patches of coarse reeds. Grey wooden bathing huts that were used for all kinds of other sports, especially after the soldiers arrived. The sand was fine and white; one could find shells that were so iridescent Nan strung them into a necklace and earrings. She went to her first dance at the Dunes Hotel, but came back a few hours later crying her eyes out. The bright-red nail varnish she'd painted the shells with had melted in the heat and run down her skin. Her peasant-style blouse was ruined. She was only fourteen. Everyone seemed to grow up quickly in the war. She insisted on leaving school, and became a Landgirl. Her dumpy little body looked comical in the baggy breeches. I went with her once or twice, to help, but those tough thistles defeated me! I think Pat must have gone to the village school – perhaps they didn't send me there because I was a cry-baby.

While wandering around a tidal pool one day I met Bill the Batman. I thought a batman was a cricketer, but he told me he was an officer's servant. He had deep-blue eyes with long black lashes, and very short black hair. He came from a big Yorkshire family, so was used to talking to small children without being patronising. We met by accident several times and I fell deeply in love. The last time it had been raining and it was cold, so I had my raincoat on over my costume. I badly needed to go home and wee, but I just wanted to stay with him for as long as possible. He told me he was being posted overseas. We shook hands solemnly. I sat on a rock and wet myself, and hoped he didn't notice.

All too soon we were shunted back to Sunderland – the idyll was over. We had to use the Morrison shelter quite often. One night there was a very close barrage and a bomb landed in the field behind our back garden. We cowered under the table, while glass from the french windows and shrapnel shattered around and over us. Upstairs a piece had been torn off all the right-hand sleeves of Mummy's coats. She was not amused.

My father was on air raid duty that night, and got back in time to help us out of the glass-strewn shelter. Apart from a few scratches we were fine, but many people were killed that night. There was an Anderson air raid shelter across the road on a piece of wasteland, but no one wanted to go there; it was mouldy, and mainly used as a toilet by vagrants and drunks.

I developed a few vices around this time. Started to smoke my father's cigars, which I filched from his desk. He caught me and made me smoke one to the end – he'd left all the doors open so I could rush to the bathroom, but stubborn little tyke that I was, I finished it and never even turned green. He was disappointed, but won in the end because I never smoked another one.

Another vice was curiosity. There was a tallboy in the sitting room, which had a locked top drawer. I found the key and climbed on a

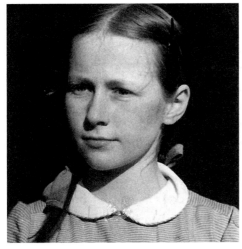

Sheila aged 10, Sunderland

Sheila aged 9

St Nicholas School, Hexham

chair. There were some strange photos of a Japanese execution. A man sat cross-legged on the ground, then in the next shot he had no head, it was in his lap, and what looked like a steel bar was sticking out of his neck ... it was blood, of course. There were also some French magazines with drawings of naked women with bare breasts and dark triangles between their legs. This I thought even stranger. I had never seen my mother in the nude, in fact it was only when I was seventeen and I opened the bathroom door unexpectedly that I saw her undressed.

Occasionally I'd pinch a few bob from her purse and use it to buy sweets, but then I saw a Japanese samurai sword in an antique shop one day and I wanted it so badly it hurt. I had a confused notion that I could defend our home against an invasion of Nazis – there were all kinds of rumours floating around, such as that Nazi paratroopers were being dropped in the countryside dressed as nuns, but we would spot them by their jackboots! So the home-made bows and arrows, which had sufficed for our gang up to then, paled beside the new concept of a real-live sword. I went in and bought it for seven and six, and in the future sought to find more, going cheap.

I was a great tree climber, frequently getting stuck and having to be rescued, hanging by my knickers. Then there was a craze for French cricket (played with a tennis racket and ball). An old lady whose garden was in the line of fire snaffled our tennis balls and wouldn't give them back. We wrote her a letter in our blood (which wasn't easy, pricking ourselves and trying to squeeze out enough blood to write a letter), saying she must give the balls back, or else, signed 'The Black Hand'. I was amazed when a policeman paid a visit to my father about his belligerent daughter, and I self-righteously said that *she* was a thief, so we were justified. I was warned about taking the law into my own hands. I had been inspired by reading the *Just William* books – that's what he would have done.

At Sunderland Primary School I was having the usual trouble with the fact that I had the wrong accent. Pat came to my rescue, but she couldn't always be there, and she went on to High School. Miss Ost was my maths teacher. She was brown, her clothes, brown, saggy, baggy knitted things, her face and fingers ditto, she smoked incessantly. So my hatred of maths became symbolised by her. The French mistress wasn't much better: she stank of garlic, had a permanent cold, and carried two bags, one for dirty hankies, one for clean ones (this was in the days before tissues).

The best time was at the farm. This was a field away from our garden. I was there every spare moment, mucking out the stables, milking cows, helping with the potato harvest. One day I was riding along on the 35-year-old cart horse pulling the potato cart, and the farmer wanted us to hurry up. So I kicked the horse, trotting along with only a piece of sacking between us. His backbone did some permanent damage to my potential marital value, I swear.

Best of all was the morning milk round. Ninky Pickersgill, a teenage opera singer in training with long red curls, drove the little trap. The back was open with a step down, and I would scoot up and down with a load of milk bottles for each house. The dainty little pony tittupped along, Ninky singing her heart out, often forgetting to stop for me, and I'd race to catch up.

Tony Briars was always visiting the farm and he became my heart's desire. He was quite kind to me, but he was all of 13 so out of my league. The farmer sent me on a mission to pick up a strawberry roan pony and her foal. She was running loose in a winter field way over the other side of town. He gave me two rope bridles and directions. Catching the pony and putting the bridle on her wasn't easy, but I managed it by climbing on a fence. The hardest part was the foal. Not used to humans, and very skittish, he didn't want to know. Somehow I managed it. It was quite late in the afternoon by the time I'd led them out of the field, closed the gate behind me, struggled on the pony's back again, and set off back to the farm. I had to cross a couple of main roads, and my pony was keen to get back to the stable so she just went across without recourse to signals. Traffic stopped wherever we went, it was like a royal progress! It was taken for granted that I would manage the task, but the farm hands winked at each other as I rode in, later than expected.

A brand new bicycle was my ninth birthday present, so new the brakes were stiff. I wanted to ride it straight away. Off I went down a cobbled side road, which led onto the main road. The brakes stuck, I careered out into the traffic and was knocked over. The driver, ashen-faced, peered over at me as I lay in the road.

'Are you all right?'

'A bit bruised, I think,' I managed to reply. A policeman turned up, they always did in those days, and my bike and I were escorted back to our house. As usual my father was furious with me. The policeman demonstrated that a child could not easily press the brake lever, so in effect it was not really my fault that I'd careered into the road, but my parents' for not oiling said brakes. In retrospect I was incredibly lucky not to be killed outright.

Wanting to give my mother a nice surprise one day, I decided to bake a cake, she was expecting guests for tea, and I knew she wouldn't be back from town in time to make anything. By this time we no longer had maids (although there was a char lady who came in once a week 'to do the rough'). The cake turned out OK, then I iced it, but there was nothing to decorate it with. I had a brilliant idea – cut up beetroot into tiny pieces, and carefully place them around the edge. Most artistic, I thought. We all sat down to tea and Mummy praised me for making the cake. On tasting it our guest looked a bit dubious, but didn't like to say anything. Mummy tasted it and gave me a funny look. Afterwards she said, 'What was that red stuff?'

'Beetroot. Well, it is sweet.'

It was then she began to think I was a bit peculiar, or maybe it was earlier...

A team of Russian dancers, the Don Cossack Choir, came to our local sports ground to promote Anglo–Russian relations. They rode on Mongol ponies, and were incredibly fit and agile, swinging under the ponies, standing on their bare backs, looking so picturesque with black fur hats, red blouson shirts, and blue baggy trousers tucked into shiny black boots. They sang 'Ochichernia', (Black eyes), and the Volga Boatmen song, and danced like dervishes, marvellous 'kazatkas', squatting and flinging out their bent legs alternately.

Margot Fonteyn and Michael Somes toured with the ballets *Swan Lake* and *Les Sylphides*, ethereal, romantic, spectacular – I was mesmerised. This is what I was going to be, but the hard part would be persuading my parents to let me take ballet classes. At age ten I was almost too old to start. It seemed positively frivolous to be thinking of a career when England was in a parlous state, with the

USA dithering about joining in the war, and the Germans bombing us to smithereens.

Stringent food and clothing rations were in force, we ate powdered eggs and whale meat, and grew our own vegetables in government-organised allotments. Gracie Fields started making patriotic films about yodelling factory girls in scarves and curlers, and Vera Lynn sang treacly songs like 'The white cliffs of Dover', and 'I'll be seeing you', and later we pirated the German song 'Lili Marlene', made famous by Marlene Dietrich.

I became fascinated by haunted houses. One of the large houses in the well-to-do part of Sunderland had been bombed early in the war, and now lay derelict. I dared my best friend Ruth to come with me, but she sensibly declined. I went there quite late one afternoon. The sun was shining on the big wrought iron gates, glinting on the few windows that were intact. The gates were unlocked. As I went up the winding driveway I felt like Pip in *Great Expectations*, creeping into the graveyard. The front door was of heavy carved oak, with a dull brass knocker. Already I wished I hadn't come. As I turned the handle the door swung open, creaking eerily. Inside was very dark, a strange smell of plaster and charcoal, a long hallway, high ceilings. It was too spooky. I turned tail and rushed out, but vowed to go back the next weekend.

This time it was early morning – what a difference! I went up the partially destroyed staircase, but stopped at the first landing, a gaping hole in front of me. I could see the roof was open to the sky two landings above. I retraced my footsteps gingerly, thought I'd try the basement but didn't have a torch, so went back to the sunlit rooms. A roundel had fallen from the ceiling, pale blue and gold, so I put it in my pocket as a souvenir. Stepping through the broken window into the back garden I was amazed – raspberries, strawberries, all ripe. I started to cram them into my mouth, we were starved of fresh fruit.

Then I saw it – a policeman's helmet on the handle of a garden spade stuck upright in the freshly turned soil. The man had stripped off his uniform top and had been digging. He shouted at me and I turned and ran through the window, spearing my knee on a swordlike piece of glass. Fortunately I had a hanky with me and bound up the flowing wound. He would have caught me, but he had to put his jacket and helmet on before he could be seen in a state of undress! My mother was unsurprised and took me to the doctor to have stitches. She was so used to my tomboy lifestyle she never queried my story that I'd fallen out of a tree.

Around this time I began to be curious about my mother's family. There were two grandparents, uncles, aunts and cousins on the Scottish side, but no one we knew about on her English side. When I quizzed her about it she told me her mother came from a well-to-do family, the Towers. She said she was a debutante and was presented at Court to Edward, the Prince of Wales. She fell in love with her groom, an unheard of social gaffe, and eloped with him. My mother Phyllis was born in Clonmel, southern Ireland. Her mother abandoned her when she was small. She said she spent half the year with her father's impoverished family (the Masons) in the East End of London, and the other half with the more upper-crust side (the Towers), in ... where? Sometimes it was Norfolk, sometimes London, or even Southsea. Aunt Lylie, a formidable dowager resembling Queen Mary, from the Norfolk branch, took Mummy under her wing and taught her some airs and graces. She never went to an ordinary school, but had a governess. She mentioned Aunt Kate and Uncle Edward Tower (we had old photos of them dated 1911), and Aunt Lylie's two daughters, Vera and Muriel.

All this seemed like a story from Victorian penny-dreadful novel. Was she illegitimate? Is that why there was such a mystery? When I asked, she refused to say any more. I didn't even know my grandmother's Christian name. This peculiar upbringing could explain why Mummy was such a snob, why the idea that I might turn into a badly-spoken yob so alarmed her. My sisters were not interested in our forebears, and knew no more than I did. It also explained why there was a constant state of war between my parents. She felt she had married beneath her. Yet he came from a very respectable middle-class Scots family. His addiction to Scotch was fuelled by her aggressive badgering when he did come home. Their rows became increasingly physical, especially after he was issued with a pistol as part of the Home Guard equipment.

She would always be on the lookout for any mention in the newspapers of Lord Greenway, who she said was a distant cousin, and she would cut out bits from the Court Circulars mentioning him. A certain Commander Bradshaw used to visit us – Mummy was barmy about the Royal Navy. His bluff and cheery presence was a tonic, as very few other people visited us because of the bitter atmosphere. We never asked school friends home for tea or to stay over.

Inevitably I came to the conclusion that my parents had never loved each other – so why get married? Did she have to get married? Would my sister Nan have been a bastard if they hadn't? Artfully I would ask Mummy how they first met. She said she was working in one of the London shops, a posh one of course, in Kensington. They 'bumped into each other'. He had curly fair hair and bright-blue eyes, was tall, wore his Merchant Navy officer's uniform with style, spoke with a soft Scots burr, and had travelled widely in the Far East – romantic. She had blue-green eyes, gently waved auburn hair, a nice slim figure, and perfect peaches and cream skin. There must have been a strong physical attraction.

Aunt Lylie felt he was an unsuitable escort and sent Phyllis away on holiday to Southsea, possibly to prevent history repeating itself. He followed her there and, having no car to take her out, got a job as a steamroller driver! He persuaded her to agree to go out on a date with him, then drove up in this quixotic contraption. Strange wooing, reminiscent of *The Taming of the Shrew*. It worked, though, and they got married, he left the navy, and found a job as an engineering rep. Then, after several babies, she was stuck in Newcastle-on-Tyne, far away from the bright lights of London.

Could her father have still been alive then? I knew he had fought in the First World War, and she showed me some medals and his dog tags, which had been cut open across the disc – did he die in the war? The answer to these questions was only partially resolved in London, on February 15th 2000 at the Public Records Office.

Miss Horobin was the headmistress of the school in Sunderland, a formidable figure. Our motto was 'The Fear of the Lord is The Beginning of Wisdom' – I was certainly terrified of her! My schoolwork was suffering from the effects of bullying by my classmates. My mother decided I must go to boarding school. Perhaps she thought I could avoid some of the terrible rows that increased in hatred with each year. She lobbied all kinds of places and eventually was advised to apply to the Reverend Eryk Agard Evans, Headmaster of St Nicholas School for Boys, Haining Croft, Hexham in Northumberland.

Normally he would only take girls of up to five years old as day pupils, and I was twelve ... but she persuaded him that I was very immature physically and not likely to be a threat to the pre-adolescent youths in his care. Because it was wartime, pre-war strictures were not so literally adhered to, and he was a kind man. I loved it there, was treated like one of the boys, and my naturally tomboyish instincts helped. I played rugby for a while, until my lousy sense of direction found me scoring a try on my own twenty-five line! Then it was 'footer', played in the quad in front of the school building with a tennis ball. My little tennis shoes were no match for the hard boots of the boys, and I gave that up too. Mr Durham taught maths; he struggled with me, but at least he taught me the rudiments of chess. Miss Alcock taught history; she was young and attractive, and she encouraged in me what would become a lifelong fascination with the past.

The uniform was grey, with a red stripe. Mine had to be invented by Mummy: a grey pleated skirt, white blouse, grey blazer edged with red, grey knee socks. Once a week I donned jodhpurs and went for riding lessons at Corbridge near Bardon Mill, an old Roman camp (Corstopitum). Jogging along beside Hadrian's Wall, I would imagine the Romans using the same tracks. Northumberland's rolling countryside is underrated and incredibly beautiful. I learned how to canter and gallop, how to jump over low logs and fences, and how to do tack – just as important as sitting correctly on a horse, as brushing and caring for your pony formed a bond, difficult enough when you only rode on a hack once a week.

I joined the choir, discovering I had a not-bad soprano voice. The Revd Eryk wore a marvellous selection of richly embroidered vestments on Sundays; he followed a High Church form of service. There was incense, sung responses, and his sermons were always interesting, often relating to the war that was so easy to forget in this peaceful area, in a lovely old cathedral near the school. During the week he wore a long black cassock, and very quiet shoes – he could sneak up on one. I adored him from the first. He taught English, scripture and Latin. We used a book called *Latin with Laughter*, illustrated with cartoons of gawky 'puellae' and hamfisted 'agricolae'. He had dark wavy hair with distinguished grey bits at the temples, a fine beaky nose, a beautiful voice, and a splendid sense of humour.

Revd Eryk had three sons, Hilary, Dik, and Christopher. Christopher was in my class, and I thought him a bit standoffish because he was the headmaster's son. He was tall for his age, plumpish, growing out of his short pants. Hilary I only saw once: it was half term, and I was sick in bed with a cold. I slept in his bedroom, so when he came home he looked there for a change of clothes. Seeing me snuffling away, he cheered me up, talking all kinds of nonsense. He was tall, and slim with a full, downturning mouth like his father. Dik was always away at school, and I only met him when I was much older. Their mother, Freda, a very clever woman, was somewhere in the south doing hush-hush work for the government.

I was a naughty little girl, quite a flirt, I used to get notes in class from a day boy, Ian Crosser, and we'd meet at the end of the garden in the bushes for some innocent kisses. One night I'd raided the next dorm for a pillow fight, it was quite late, and we didn't hear the Revd's soft footfall. He swooped down on us and I, as the ringleader, was hauled off to his study. He gave me a stern lecture on disobedience, then allowed me to choose – his hairbrush or a gym shoe. I chose the latter (it sounded softer). He put me over his knee, smoothed my nightie over my bottom, and gave me three solid whacks. It hurt a lot, but being so close to him was bliss.

We had moved to a much bigger house in Sunderland, and seemed to do a lot of entertaining. Nan was now one of the youngest girls in the WRENS. She camped outside Rear Admiral Tower's office for a week until he allowed her to be posted overseas to Alexandria as a signals operator, presumably on the strength of their distant relationship! Once there she had the unenviable distinction of being propositioned by King Farouk in a nightclub. Which, I hasten to say, she turned down.

Towards the end of the year Revd Eryk wrote a special pantomime, and I was given a big part in it. I was my first experience of the warm glow of appreciation and applause from an audience. Admittedly a captive audience of friends and parents! By this time he was obliged to tell my mother that she would have to find another school for me as I was growing up too fast ... or so he inferred. The event he feared only happened at the age of 15.

My next school was an Anglican convent: St Hilda's School, Sneaton Castle, at Whitby. At first I hated it, found it hard to make friends, and resented the intrusive religiosity. By the time I had found a friend and got used to an all girls' school, my mother had given notice and I had to leave again at the end of the year. Several things stand out. The sadness of seeing beautiful girls, with lovely blonde hair, becoming withdrawn postulants, their locks shorn off, hidden beneath caps tied under the chin, eyes downcast, and later novices, shut away from the normal world, given to God.

There was one long weekend, when one of my friends was visited by a so-called 'cousin'. He brought booze, cigarettes, and was closeted away with one or more of her friends, lots of smothered giggles going on behind the door. I wasn't included, I was far too young-looking, no breasts, nothing to appeal to the man, luckily!

I refused to be confirmed, stating I would do so once I was old enough to make a considered decision. The bishop was furious with me. I didn't want his disgusting old hands on me. One day we were given cornflakes for breakfast instead of grey cardboard-looking wheat flakes. Mother Superior clapped her hands for silence. She said the war in Europe was over. We looked at each other, should we cheer? A prayer was said instead.

One of the nuns taught me to swim at long last, at a seawater pool near Whitby. She gave me the confidence to float on my back, and once I could do that it was no time before I could swim a breadth. We went on lovely picnics on the moors, but we had to eat awful pork pies full of disgusting uncooked white goo and jelly. The food was usually terrible, grey meat in huge tasteless pies or stews, things like tapioca, (frog spawn) and semolina.

During the holidays I realised the war really was over. Men in badly-fitting blue demob suits were everywhere, there was a marvellous sense of relief, no blackout on the windows at night, street parties, and, sadly, crippled young men, covered in fresh bandages, begging on street corners. Rationing would continue for some years, but we were nowhere near starving ... unlike parts of Europe and Russia. My mother tried to hide away the sickening newspaper photos of piles of the dead, and the skeletal survivors from Dachau, Auschwitz and Belsen-Buchenwald, but they were everywhere, even on the news reels in the cinema.

I started to have ballet classes. My teacher Margaret Cross, an ex-dancer, said it wasn't too late, but most people thought you had to start at about five years old to be any good. I was desperate to succeed, but my limbs tended to let me down, particularly my ankles. Back at school I was in the long-jumping team and, as a 'reward for good behaviour' was allowed to polish the chapel floor. Next thing I had water on the knee, or as it's unromantically called, 'housemaids knee'. Antiphlogestin poultices (bright yellow horrors) were applied. Years later while dancing in *Canterbury Tales* my knees were locking, and X rays showed some broken pieces of bone which periodically lodged in the cartilage behind the kneecap, relics of the exertions at St Hilda's!

The school put on an outdoor performance of *Hiawatha*. Most of us were just capering Red Indians/choir, slathered with brown body paint, the prefects playing the leads, but the poetry and music captivated me. In retrospect I think it was a very special occasion. We sang the Crucifixion oratorio, the 'Stabat Mater' as well, but that was too static for me.

Some of my classmates were the daughters of West African chiefs, and I had my first taste of multi-racial mixing. Our school sent out missionaries to Africa, and these girls were sent back in exchange, so to speak. They were gregarious and we liked them as individuals, so there was never any resentment. I was known as 'Fergy'. No one had ever liked me enough to give me a nickname before. I even had a best friend who wrote to me after I left – but it all happened too late.

Sneaton Castle was a strange mixture – Victorian Gothic, with a huge banqueting hall where we ate and had meetings – but St Hilda's original settlement, the Abbey, stood alone on the headland, very little of it remaining. We were taught to be proud of her example, one of the earliest feminists. Walking along the beach we would be on the lookout for ammonites, a fossil in a shell shape, which had been her symbol, and was on the school badge.

Whitby has two reasons for its renown: Dracula is reputed to have sailed there from Transylvania, and there is a thriving tourist trade connected with this, although back in 1946, no one seemed to be aware of it. The other was the mining of jet – so fashionable in Victoria's last years, she would wear no other ornament, and it became de rigueur for fashionable matrons.

The village was backed onto the cliffside, appearing vertical. Most dwellings were painted white with black timbering, no pastel colours in that harsh windy climate. Visitors would be encouraged to take us out to Robin Hood's Bay along the coast. Long sweeping sands, wonderful seascapes. Or drive inland onto the moors, have picnics among the gorse and wild bluebells and a pervasive acrid sheep smell.

My next school was near Lake Windermere in Westmoreland (now part of Cumbria). St Anne's-on-Sea was evacuated there early in the war. It had been a private estate, a fine grey stone mansion with vast stretches of lawn, tennis courts, pergolas and well-kept flower beds. True to form, the playing fields were miles away. We walked everywhere in crocodiles, two by two, and it was difficult for a new girl who started halfway through the year to find a partner. Once again starting from scratch to make friends, I suddenly realised that I couldn't be bothered with this aspect of school life, the triviality, pettiness and regimentation. Once I no longer really cared to make an impression, life became easier.

I would deliberately walk on my own, or with the gym mistress, a slightly shop-worn blonde with bulging blue eyes who was a frequent visitor to the Rising Sun in Grasmere. For a while I had a crush on her, but her alcoholic/peppermint aroma reminded me too much of my father. A skinny twelve-year-old with long curly ringlets, big blue eyes and a defenceless full mouth was in the class below me. I fancied her rotten, and I think it was returned, but then we had a school dance – meandering around to gramophone records – and I asked her to dance. She was so nervous she farted when we held each other in a clammy-handed foxtrot – somehow that killed the romance before it even started.

Swimming sessions were a frightening experience. My confidence began to ooze away once in the freezing dark waters of the lake. Reeds dragged at my feet, cramp took hold, the bank seemed very far away ... it was October, for God's sake! An old crone appeared saying, 'Boveril or caw caw?' She had such a strong accent it took me a while to grasp that we were being offered hot drinks.

There was a strong divide between the ordinary Cumbrian girls and the rich pretty ones with 'county' connections. I had always scorned my mother's snobbery, but now at least I could hold my own as far as speech and good manners were concerned, thanks to her. Secretly I was determined to go my own way, no matter what society dictated. I began reading voraciously, Dickens, Dostoevsky, Chekov, Steinbeck, Upton Sinclair. One day, lying on my back under the huge leafless elm trees, I began to fantasise about the twig patterns ... what if all the ends connected to something in outer space? I tried to imagine it, but it was like visualising the size of the universe.

We went to visit the Brontë vicarage at Haworth. No curtains on the windows, tiny rooms looking out over the graveyard where three of the family were already interred. I sympathised so much with the sisters, three like us (except for the raffish Branwell). Reading *Jane Eyre* I wondered at a society that would go to such lengths to hide a mad person away instead of finding treatment for her. *Wuthering Heights* also exposed the hypocrisy of that era. Jane Austen's novels, Mrs Gaskell's *Cranford* ... I longed to be able to write a novel that would expose the cheating lifestyle, the 'keeping up appearances' of my mother's class.

A craze developed: glassy-glassy, played in the dark, with fingers on the glass, asking unanswerable questions. We didn't have an ouija board, but it worked sporadically, enough to frighten us. Then there was the Bible trick: a key twisted with string and hung in the air from the Bible; the way it twirled indicated yes or no. They asked, 'Will I have babies?', 'Will I have a handsome lover?' Influenced by Emily Brontë I began to write rather abstruse would-be mystical poetry. I had a recurring vision of a black meadow, I would be at the lower part looking up a steep hill to a sliver of moonlit horizon. Something in the future...

We had absolutely terrifying storms, which have only been matched in my experience by the Wagnerian African storms. I felt as though we should run for the air raid shelter. Once or twice I had to restrain myself from hiding under the bed – only the thought of the ridicule of my peers prevented me acting out this fear.

Pat had given me a leather-bound copy of Shelley for my birthday, so I was influenced by his high-flown style, Keats and Byron were to be next. Maths was as ever the bane of my life, I didn't mind algebra, it seemed logical, and geometry involved drawing, but plain arithmetic, those ridiculous problems! I mean, who cares if two men are rolling a stone up a hill, or how long it takes? Art and English, with history and biology, were my favourite subjects. The maths mistress, a plain jolly-hockey-sticks female, told me I lacked self-discipline.

Quite by accident I was asked to read a Shakespeare speech aloud in class. It made absolute sense to me, and the emotions aroused were of a startling intensity (usually these speeches were read in a lack-lustre sing-song which rendered the content meaningless). These were supposedly adult emotions, but I knew them, they were mine. It was very exciting, like discovering a secret password to the future. I wanted to tell Pat about it, but she was away from home, studying art at Durham University. Both my parents had a talent for drawing, as I did, but she was the most talented.

Valerie Bayne and I became friends. She was a sweet-natured girl from Barrow-in-Furness. I went to stay with her one long weekend, and for the first time was accepted into a normal, happy family, who laughed and joked unselfconsciously. We did the usual things: picnics and a visit to the rose-stone Furness Abbey, almost completely destroyed during the reign of Henry VIII, but with enough left of the majestic nave to be able to visualise its former glory.

It was a Church of England school, so on Sundays we did the eternal crocodile walk to church. I was so bored with the sermons, and the solid hassocks were giving my susceptible knees a hard time. A friend was a Methodist. She said the sermons were short and you didn't have to kneel. Also – no crocodile. We both went to Chapel from then on.

Then it was over. Once again my mother had given notice, without any explanation. I had come to love the Lake District, particularly with all the literary connections around us. Valerie and I corresponded for a while, but I didn't keep it up, what was the point? I found out my father had lost his cushy wartime job and we were in dire financial straits. They'd moved back to Newcastle, and were living in a top-floor flat in Osborne Road.

Nan had a secretarial job at the university, and was going out with a Sikh. I thought him very handsome and exotic with his nice clean turban. He used to sing 'Money is the root of all evil', in a Peter Sellers way (long before 'Goodness gracious me!'). For a while there was no school for me. It never occurred to anyone that my mother could get a job – she was only forty-six after all! She and I met her friend Elsie for coffee one day at a rather downmarket place where we had to queue. I had a book with me and was reading it. Mummy said it was rude of me to read. For some reason I felt this was the last straw and flounced out. It was all so pointless, no money, no school, no future. I hated them both at that moment.

There was a flowering bush in the garden – deadly nightshade. I took some of the berries upstairs with me, swallowed them and lay down to die! Mummy arrived home, saw me lying there and was irritated.

'Why did you walk out like that, it was so embarrassing. Get up at once and make the tea!'

'I'm not getting up, I'm dying.' I lay there with my hands crossed over my breast (I couldn't understand why I was still conscious). What a drama queen. After a few questions she realised I might be telling the truth and went into a terrible flap. I explained that I'd swallowed the berries whole, without chewing them. She made me put my finger down my throat, drink salt water, but nothing came up. Then she had to be comforted, and some of the strain she was under penetrated my thick selfish skull. We had a cup of tea and talked about something else. I was fine ... heaven knows why I wasn't dead, perhaps that bush wasn't poisonous after all.

Mummy began to suffer dreadfully from tinnitus, constant ringing in the ears, also brought on by stress, I suppose. One night I sat stroking her forehead and praying hard to Someone to take it away. The next day the noise had gone, miraculously. My father had applied for a job with the Control Commission in Germany, and was there being interviewed. Without the money for fees, Pat was forced to leave university, had a frightful row with Mummy, and rushed off to join the ATS. She had flat feet, so I don't understand why they accepted her. It helped with space, however, as we were squashed into two rooms and a shared bathroom.

The Wicherskis lived in the adjoining flat. He had been a pilot with the Polish Airforce, had come to the UK when the Nazis overran Poland and flew with the RAF. He was so dashing in his uniform with the flowing cape. I had a crush on him of course, but he was married to an English girl and they had a tiny baby. Sometimes I babysat for them, but the little dear never woke up, so it was an easy couple of hours. Another married couple asked if I would do the same with their son of 18 months. He did wake up and wanted to wee – he was a boy, and I had never been asked to give a boy a potty. I took his nappy off, then was nonplussed. I said, 'I don't know what to do!'

'Yew doan knaw what te dew?' he repeated in an incredulous Scots voice. I handed him the potty and he held it in front of him. I helped him hold it and he duly pissed into it.

'See!'

Well, I really lost face. But I learned something useful.

Nan had a new boyfriend, Bill Eldon: a Byronic figure, curly brown hair, blue-green eyes, aristocratic profile, and affected a silver-knobbed cane. He was a medical student at St Bartholomew's Hospital in London. I thought he was wonderful, but he didn't know I existed, or so I thought.

We still had a few first editions. Most of them had been sold to help pay the rent. I clung onto the last set – leather-bound, gilt-edged, sepia-speckled plays, with hand-tinted illustrations of actors playing Shakespearean parts, Mrs Siddons as Volumnia in contemporary crinoline, David Garrick as Hamlet. But then we had to part with them. A telegram came from Daddy: he'd got the job. We moved into the Regent Hotel preparatory to joining him. Things were looking up!

1948

After the war I started keeping a diary, so now I am not relying solely on memory.

January 1948 – The railways are nationalised. We sell our valuable stamps and the last of the first editions. We go to the first night of *Peter Pan* with Phyllis Calvert and Peter Murray-Hill. It's freezing, but our wardrobe is locked and we have to go out without coats.

29th February – Leap year, Daddy's birthday but he's in Germany. I have my second innoculation preparatory to travelling to Germany. On the 8th March I go to see Richard Todd and Phyllis Calvert in a play, *An Ideal Husband*, it's very good. The Polish premier Jan Masaryk commits suicide. He was a charismatic war hero. On the 18th the Queen arrives in Newcastle, she is lovely, and very serene.

22nd March – The bank manager tells us we have no money. Send an urgent telegram to Daddy! There are some Indians in the hotel and they ask us to come for tea. It's horrible, made with ghee and condensed milk. Daddy phones to say he has suspected diphtheria. A strange sight on April 1st in Osborne Road – a tram catches fire.

2nd April – We set off. Get up at 5.30 and catch the 8.00 train to London. We are supposed to meet Pat at Kings Cross station, but she's not there – we post her suitcase on to her. We catch a taxi and ride through the poorer parts of London. Then onto the Underground. I'm very nervous, first time on an escalator. Tea at Marshall and Snelgrove's. Afterwards there's a terrible downpour while we're waiting for a bus, and we're soaked. I catch sight of St Paul's through the rain, am not impressed! Catch the boat train to Harwich and have a meal at the hotel with the other families. Pass Customs without incident and board the SS *Arnhem*, supposed to be a luxury ship.

A terrific gale blows up during the night, but I'm not sick. I love it, I go up on deck and ride the storm. Arrive at the Hook of Holland in the morning. We're taken to a Transit Camp and have breakfast. Buy sweets and biscuits for the train. We catch the CCG train (Control Commission), enchanted by the flat Dutch landscape. Tulips and windmills! Met by Daddy at Herford. Our first ride in a Volkswagen. Staying in Detmold in Westphalia, at the United Services Club until our flat is ready.

8th April – We move into the flat. Ilse our maid is nice. The furniture is ugly Utility stuff. I join the library, it's 2.36 pfennigs. We now use BAFS (British Forces 'funny money').

10th April – Nan arrives (she gets a job as a secretary at Bad Hermannsborn – a secret service hideout). We go to the Officers Club Dance. Next day we walk to the top of Hermannsdenkmal (statue). It's a huge bronze, and apparently he was a German who was trained as a soldier by the occupying Romans, then he came back helped to vanquish the Romans. So he's a great hero.

18th April – Go for a walk with Ann Dyer, and see a chimney sweep, he's black from top to toe! It's supposed to be very lucky to see one. I go riding most days, but only along restricted paths.

1st May – Dinner Dance at the Club. I wear my new long pink dress (bought with coffee and cigarettes on the black market).

7th May – I start my new school today. King Alfred's School, Plön, Schleswig Holstein. Arrive at 12.30 pm. I am in 5b. This is a wonderful place. The lake is beautiful, we're allowed to go sailing once we can swim five lengths. I can swim a breadth! The pool is an enclosed part of the jetty. Miss Richardson is our Housemistress (Temple). I'm a Helper, or Prefect.

19th May – There are some really nice boys here. We go out of the school for the first time – the countryside is beautiful, lots of birch woods and lakes. I have my first shower, love it! Marks for exams – English – 78%, General Knowledge – 81%, Maths – 3%!

Sailing in Nordeney, 1948

Daddy

My first party dress in BAOR

Nan

Pat in a play

Sunday 23rd May – We all go to see the headmaster (Freddy Spencer Chapman, who wrote 'The Jungle is Neutral' about his war experiences in Burma with General Orde Wingate, and who climbed in Tibet). He's a very attractive man, curly brown hair, expressive eyes, but with scars on his face from his time in Burma. He reminds me a little of Eryk Evans. I am made a librarian. We ask questions about the reason for, and the running of, the school. It was a naval training base before we took it over, and has five conjoined lakes.

29th May – Pat's birthday. We have a school social. I like David Truscott. He's known as 'coppernob'. A slightly Somerset accent. I teach him to waltz. He waits for me after breakfast the next day. We go to a concert at Plön in the old church. 'The Day of Judgement', angelic voices. By Bach, I think.

3rd June – Art class. I meet the new art master Mr Heriz-Smith. I stay behind after class and we talk about art, acting, books, everything – it's an apocalypse. Found a kindred spirit! David and I go down to the beach. He takes photos of Pat (another Pat), Peter and me. We go behind a rock. He puts his arm around me and kisses me, my first kiss from a boy! But he smells funny, metallic. I suppose it's romantic.

Saturday 5th June – Go fishing and are caught in a rainstorm. See a dreadful film, *Merton of the Movies*. David sits beside me, puts his arm around me and holds my hand. He's assumed possession of me, so to speak. I quite like him, but there are others I like better. I give him a photo of me in my party frock.

6th June – Have decided that, although I like him very much, he's not my type. I don't much like kissing him. His teeth are rather dirty – greenish coloured. I'd rather be 'A Cat that walks by itself' (Kipling). Have told him, though not why, and we are still friends.

11th June – Our cricket and rounders team beat Hamburg. Gramophone recital in the evening. Patrick Heriz-Smith plays 'Façade', the ballet music, wonderful. I am going to produce and act in the G.B. Shaw play *Androcles and the Lion*. I'll be playing Androcles.

Saturday 3rd July – I go sketching beside the lake. Patrick and the Dr glide up in a canoe. Record concert in the evening, he plays Beethoven's Fifth Symphony, I'm ecstatic! Meeting with Freddy and Trevelyan, British Forces Director of Education. He discourses on Attitude to Work and Tradition. This is a peculiar school, as we have Canadians, Americans, Yugoslavs, French, etc, but we all get on well.

Am reading Karl Marx, *The Socialist Sixth of the World*, and *Best Detective Stories*. My class grade is A minus. Patrick tells me I must do as he says (a shiver runs down my spine as I imagine what he might tell me to do). He means I mustn't destroy my drawings, even when I think they are bad. Our team come back from our sister school Prince Rupert's at Willemshaven. They didn't win anything but had a good time at the dance afterwards!

Go swimming. Mrs Potter, the beautiful wife of Captain Potter, Nan's boss, takes a photo of me in my grey and green waffle costume. I discover it's see-through when wet, very embarrassing. I'm afraid to get out of the pool. Patrick's concert in the evening, 'Fingal's Cave' (Mendelssohn), and 'Nutcracker Suite (Tchaikovsky).

Saturday 12th June – Many parents came today, but not mine. (It's a 12-hour journey by train). Sylvia Harvey's parents take me out to Kiel. We have a lovely time, superb meals. I catch a glimpse of the Baltic Sea through the entrance to Kiel harbour. The sterns of bombed ships are sticking up out of the water.

Monday, I help the School Librarian sort out books. He is a sweet, cultured old man. I am beginning to revise my ideas about Germans. Tuesday is a school holiday. We go by bus to Sir Malcolm Sergeant's concert at Kiel. They play Benjamin Britten's 'Child's Guide to the Orchestra', based on a theme by Purcell. It starts with one instrument and gradually, separately, the others join in, in a swelling crescendo, very inspiring. We go to the beach at Erkenfurder, picnic, and bathe

King Alfred's School, Plön

in the Baltic. There is so much salt in the water you can float very easily, like lying on a mattress!

Sat 19th June – I get the Art Room keys from Patrick Heriz-Smith, and paint on my own. Take them back to his flat. I try to look in but don't get any further than the doorway; his plump, red-haired wife blocks the way. I wish I could see his paintings – if any?

26th June – See *Les Miserables*, it's very good. Patrick signs my autograph book, a beautifully artistic signature. I love the aquiline shape of his nose, which has a slightly retroussé tip.

My marks from exams are: French 25 out of 31, Maths D, German B, (3 As, 3 Bs, 1 D). Temple (my House) lose athletics, but are third in the swimming. I'm the official runner and have fun taking the results to the judges. Am reading *Babbitt* by Upton Sinclair, and *Everybody's Pepys*, *Stray Lamb* by Thorne Smith, and *Women* by Winifred Holtby. Dress rehearsal of *Androcles and the Lion* goes off quite well.

Saturday 17th July – Concert by a dancer, Paola Manucci. Some dances very good, costumes effective. Sunday, Patrick's concert: 'Eine Kleine Nachtmusik', Mozart, Schubert's Unfinished Symphony, 'Vandenberg Concerto'. He smiles at me, how I adore him!

20th July – Biology 83% (1st), Geography 54% (?), German 63% (8th). I start a landscape in Patrick's room, 'The Pond'.

21st July – Prince Rupert School teams are visiting us. We compete with them at sports and swimming. I carry on painting my landscape. Dance in the evening. I dance with Gusty (Donald Gustavson the Canadian), Donald Berry, John Reece and Pedder. The buffet is superb. There's a thunderstorm, afterwards the sky is a gorgeous peachy red.

Friday 23rd July – We win the riding tournament. I give in my library books and say goodbye to Herr Jager. He has delightful old-world manners. We give Miss Richardson, our Housemistress, a birthday party. Flowers, jelly, a cake with rum in it! Patrick's concert in the evening. 'Spitfire Prelude and Fugue (Walton), 'Peter and the Wolf' (Prokoviev), and 'Petrouchka' (Stravinsky). Exam results: English 72% (2nd), History 72% (3rd), Maths brings down my average as always. Final Grade 63% (4th).

Sat 24th July – Holidays. Go home to Detmold by train.

Mon 2nd August – Mummy, Daddy and I go by train to Nordeney (Frisian Islands, near Denmark). It's very hot at first, but cools down when we reach the sea. Cross by ferry. First thing we see is a giant crane. Daddy says it's for seaplanes. We are staying at the Kaiserhof Hotel.

Wednesday 4th August – We go to a celebrity concert by pianist and cellist, Professor Pollack. Next night it's the 'Nordeney Hayride'!

Ferdinando Luisi and Maria Corelli sing well, the 'Hiller Girls' dance competently, but the comedians are awful, one is a circus clown who laughs maniacally while playing an ear-splitting musical saw. I've never liked clowns, find them frightening and unfunny.

We go sailing and swimming. The baths have artificial waves every half hour, a novelty. It's very picturesque here, the men wear mostly skull caps and bathing robes, mainly tanned and handsome, the girls pretty. There are horse-drawn four-wheeler cabs, and even the buses are horse-drawn. Mummy is in hospital in Copenhagen with a sprained ankle. Daddy and I go to the cabaret in the evening, I wear my long pink dress, and afterwards we play skittles at the English-style pub downstairs; you can even play darts and shove ha'penny.

We ride out on hired bicycles. It's very windy. Meeting Mummy's ship at the quayside a real storm whips up, it's high tide and the harbour is flooded, but her ship docks all right and she's much better.

I go sailing and swimming with Madeleine and Jean-Pierre Villemer, who are staying in our hotel. It's choppy, and am feeling quite seasick, and glad to reach land! Riding again with the MO (Medical Officer) who attended to Mummy's ankle. He's very nice. I fall off Sultan when he trips, but it's deep silvery sand and I'm none the worse.

Friday 13th August – We leave Nordeney. I've bought a silver bracelet and a little black rubber witch with bendy legs and arms, christened it 'Patrick'.

Various cocktail parties follow, and I meet Tony Gow-Smith. He's a Naval Cadet Officer, tall, blond wavy hair, blue eyes, nice voice ... He takes me out to dinner at the CandM (an army hotel), then we go to see 'Hellsapoppin' at the local fleapit. We hold hands. He walks me home. On the way he suddenly stops and takes me in his arms. We are both shaking. He kisses me expertly ... my knees are weak!

Wednesday 25th August – Dinner at the Officers Club. Tony comes along afterwards. He looks dashing in his naval togs. We dance a

42

lot, he's very good. We meet up with a whole lot of Danish officers, and ride home with them in their Jeeps!

Saturday 28th August – Dinner at the US Club. Nan and Ann Dyer are in the party. We dance with the Danes. Mine is 6ft 6ins tall, Anders von Buchwald, of German descent. We do waltzes, tangos, foxtrots, quicksteps. At 1pm the band plays 'Happy Birthday'. Hooray! I'm sixteen at last! Next day I'm given a sewing box that opens out in layers, a pearl necklace, a nylon hairbrush. I give Nan her belated present – Worth's 'Dans le Nuit'. I go for a walk with Tony. My report arrives, quite gratifying.

1st September – Go riding in the morning. The class is taken by Herr Fasse, ex trainer of the Lippizaner Greys, I practise jumping. Go to the Club. We see the Danes for the last time. Anders and I exchange addresses. We go home and I sit in the back with him. They all crowd into our flat for tea.

Thursday, go to stay with Nan at Bad Hermannsborn. She tells me why it's so hush-hush. Most thrilling. See 'Monsieur Verdoux' (Charlie Chaplin), with the Potters. Mrs Potter is wildly beautiful – a lush mouth like Rita Hayworth, long thick wavy brown hair with an exciting white streak, high cheekbones, and a marvellous figure after three children! Friday, it rains heavily all morning. I take a large poodle for a walk (Bouvier). Don't go near the Kurhaus because of the secret … we go out fox shooting in the evening. Lie in a swamp for hours, no sign of a fox.

Saturday 4th September – Back home again. The Gow-Smiths invite us to dinner at the US Club. I dance nearly every dance with Tony. Mummy is at home with a bad chill. (I seem to have been to bed after midnight every night!) The parents off to Dusseldorf. Helga the maid says she doesn't want to sleep in the attic, so I am alone. Spend the day sewing and mending. Tony goes back to England on Sunday. Next few days spent mostly riding.

Friday 10th September – Back at school. There is a new House, Fleming.

Tuesday 14th September – Go sailing with Tessa. Learn how to tie a figure-of-eight and a reef knot. We race and come in last, but it's great fun! We are weighed – am 58 something kg and 64 and a half ins. tall. A great many people in the school have pains, the runs, and flu. Am feverishly attempting to complete a watercolour landscape for the Churchill competition. Meet a nice boy called Harrington. Jane Arnot and I walk out of a stupid film, *Blockheads*. The sky is magnificent – cobalt and turquoise.

19th September – Feel shivery all day. Taken to hospital with a high temperature. Have gastric flu. Doctor comes and taps me all over. The German nurses are nice. Throat is sore and I have to have a steam inhalant basin under my nose. Wish I could have a letter from home.

23rd September – Leave hospital. Patrick says, 'Sometimes it's better to succumb.' What does he mean? Wish I had the daring to follow it up. Letter and parcel from Mummy. Tessa and I go sailing, quite a gale springs up.

Saturday 25th September – Miss Richardson tells me I am to leave the school, no reason given, Mummy phoned Freddy S. Chapman last night. I don't want to leave, especially as my best friend Paula Crowhurst arrived back at the school last night. I'm afraid I'll never get School Certificate.

26th September – Paula and I go to a concert at Fleming House (where Patrick lives). 'Don Giovanni' and 'The Messiah'. Afterwards Patrick takes me to his flat and introduces me to his wife. We talk about St Hilda's School, she went there as well. He says he wishes I wasn't going.

Ian Hamilton fetches me in a super sports car, we fairly whizz along! I catch the train to Detmold at Hamburg. I still don't know why I had to leave – lack of money again, I suppose?

30th September – Daddy and I go shooting in the evening. No luck but have a lovely time. See a squirrel and some rabbits in the woods. Mummy and I go to a symphony concert, 'Fantasie für Orchestra' by Hans Pfitzner. Beethoven's 'Pastorale', and a piano concerto, played by Detmold Municipal Orchestra.

Saturday 2nd October – Brindlay-Clarke's wedding. Afterwards Mummy and I go to the CMS Hotel. Wormald, Daddy's boss, comes and sits with us. He's most objectionable, drunk, and using the most disgusting language. We walk out.

Wednesday 6th October – Letters from Paula and Anders von Buchwald. He writes charmingly. We go to the CCG shop. I get fur-lined over-boots and a raincoat. Am reading *No Son of Mine* by G.B. Stern and *I, Claudius* by Robert Graves. I write to Pat and Anders. Go round the art gallery, impressionist nudes by Seifert, landscapes by Prof. Kuttner. Also miniatures and diamond jewellery. Mummy makes me a new frock, stone and flame, in long 'New Look' style.

Monday 11th October – Daddy takes me with him to Essen in the Ruhr, to the A.G. Farben Bunne works. We bat along the autobahn and just miss a bridge under repair. I see Volkswagen bodies being dipped into a huge vat of black paint, they do it three times. Lunch at the Essenerhof Hotel.

Thursday 14th October – Get drawing paper from Hedley. My syllabus has not arrived yet. (Now the plan is to study at home.) Am reading *John Brown's Body* by Stephen Benet, *Tales of Terror and The Supernatural* from the library, and bought *The Complete Works of Shakespeare* in one volume.

We give a cocktail party to members of Daddy's branch, including the Ketleys, Lees, Carey (the artist), and Thextons. The Brigadier couldn't come, but we had about 25 types to feed and supply with drinks. The CCG shop came to the rescue. Afterwards we went to have coffee at the New Club, and found everyone there from our party! We, of course, were stuffed with cheese straws and sausage rolls. On Sunday Daddy and I go shooting with Lee and Thexton,

Herman's Denkmal

Moscow conference,
Remscheid, 1947

Horse-riding in Germany, 1948

Hill House, Plön

[Far right]
Sheila at Hannover Zoo

the latter shoots two hares. We visit a German cottage, spotless and well-furnished.

Mummy and I go to Hobart Barracks to see Capt. Bucknell and Maj. Weston. We have an art class with Herr Fischer-Credo. And next day, another art class. It stinks! So does Herr F.C., of garlic. I'm copying an old master ... then he makes me copy grey plaster casts of hands and feet, in pencil. Says I have a perfect left third finger, I'm so thrilled.

Friday 22nd October – Have a French lesson with a young man of 18 – he seems to be only one lesson ahead of me. Dinner at the 'Duck and Catch It', as Daddy calls the CMS Hotel. He is revoltingly drunk.

Sunday 25th October – Rehearsal of *The Mikado* at the Shutzenhof in Herford. I'm in the chorus. Saturday, another rehearsal. There is a nice young Captain Dunn, with a pipe and a huge St Bernard! We are given fans to practice with. Beginning to feel quite Japanese, coyly hiding behind it.

2nd November – Another art lesson. Letter from Pat, she's been in hospital in London with bronchitis for 14 days. Uncle Andrew phones from UK to say she's been discharged.

Sat 5th November – Another letter from Pat, she's much more cheerful. Dance at the US Club. I dance with Capt. Bucknell. Nan wears a lovely white red-spotted voile dress bought at a German second-hand shop for coffee and cigarettes.

28th November – Pat arrives, she's very thin. First night of *The Mikado*. Great success. I was promoted to the front row of the chorus! Also had to sing the high notes of the 'Tit-willow' song. A salacious fellow insisted on putting his hands around my chest to help me with the highest notes! A kind of pre-Heimlich manoeuvre!

No more entries till 24th December. It's very cold, a slight amount of snow falls.

Saturday 25th December – Xmas Day. I get a Biro, a pair of silk stockings, lots of cosmetics, a bag, and perfume from Nan, 'Le Dandy D'Orsay'.

Sunday 26th December – Go to the Potters at Bad Hermannsborn. Return to Detmold and dine with Grenadier Guards officers. Peter 'Straw' Delahay, Charles Ross, he is a superb dancer, wavy blond hair, blue eyes, he likes art, acting, I like him very much. His friend, Sam, is also one of the party. We are invited to the Waterloo Ball on New Year's Eve. This is the social event of the year.

30th December – In bed with a bad cold.

Friday 31st December – Wake up in the morning. My left arm is numb. Daddy thinks I'm faking for some reason and sticks a needle into my arm – I feel nothing. I have a sort of feverish flu. Dr Thompson (the one we knew in Nordeney) comes and examines me. Thank goodness it was him, and not some old bungler. He is au fait with the latest medical developments, having recently completed his internship. He says I have poliomyelitis. (It used to be known as infantile paralysis. Many of my school friends have caught it, some died, some crippled for life. They say it's from swimming pools.) Doses me with M&B pills.

I go in an ambulance to hospital.

1949

Saturday 1st January 1949 – End up in the isolation ward at Rinteln RAF Hospital. Am alone except for a huge iron lung, which will breathe for me if the disease spreads to my lungs. [The Salk vaccine had not yet been discovered.] The nurses are very kind. Peter Arnot sends a note from school. Friends from school send me flowers, fruit and books. I can see birch trees flickering out of the window.

Rinteln Isolation War RAF Hospital (The Iron Lung),
January 1949

The room was high, cool and green
As they wheeled me in.
The bed was thin, hard and white
Under the light.

The room was high, cool and green
And indecently clean,
But I was hot, wet, in pain
Not quite the same.

A monster crouched in wait
Porthole maw – sans sate,
See how it yaws,
A coffin with paws.

Glass eyes on stilts
Expectantly tilts,
Snaky tail in a bin
All – luring me in...

Poem written in hospital, 1949

The leaves of young birch
Are swaying and caressing
With a sound of snow softly falling.

A breeze blows them
Like a flock of pale birds
A dainty mosaic of slender stems.

Next a fierce gust
Makes them imperious
Giddily delirious ... then goes.

Sunday 2nd January – Bad night. Dr Thompson comes to see me. I'm writing with my right hand.

22nd January – Visits from family. Letters from cousin Vera Wortley (Tower) and Elsie Coulson (Mummy's best friend). Third week over, thank God! The Bishop of Jarrow inspects the hospital, a sweet old man in black gaiters and a cummerbund. Someone's sent me a lovely pot of pink cyclamen, it's beside my bed. A new male nurse gives me a blanket bath. He's Scots, dark-haired. It's very cold outside. I read a great deal. Don't think about the future, or what is wrong with me, I escape into books.

26th January – Mummy and Daddy come with magazines and fruit. Letter from Eryk Evans, he suggests I convalesce at Ridley Hall (where the school has moved to), bless him!

27th January – Moved out of isolation to the families' ward. My room is fumigated. The other people in the ward are very kind, especially Mrs Clothier, she's great fun! M and D visit, there's a Prospectus from RADA arrived – I've virtually blackmailed them into promising that if and when I recover they will let me go to RADA, if I can pass the audition. Letter from Jane Arnot.

3rd February – My arm is better! When I was having physiotherapy with the electric buzzers on my arm, she told me to try to move my fingers – I tried very hard, and, miraculously the second finger of my left hand wiggled slightly! She said the nerves were regenerating, and she was as excited as I was. The parents have moved to Hannover, so can't see me as often as before. Another letter from Revd Evans, and from Patrick Heriz-Smith. I reply 'toot sweet'! Hope they'll be able to understand my right-handed scrawl.

Moved to Hannover Hospital, am sorry to leave Rinteln, where I had made some friends. It's dark and foggy. Mummy and Nan visit me. I GET UP FOR THE FIRST TIME!

7th February – Discover Donald Gustavson is also in the hospital with polio. He's in a wheelchair, his limbs are very wasted. He was such an athletic boy. He thinks he caught it at the swimming gala against Prince Rupert's School. I am very lucky, to get off so lightly. Have physio – rather painful. Parents visit. I receive a splint. It's an unwieldy metal arm, quite heavy, with webbing over it. My arm sticks out at an acute angle!

Saturday 12th February – Leave hospital. We go to see the musical *Me and My Girl*, with Lupino Lane. It's quite good, that's the one with the 'Lambeth Walk' in it. We are staying at a hostel in Eckerman Strasse. Hannover is quite pleasant. My arm is steadily improving.

15th February – Daddy in bed with flu. Nan goes back to UK tomorrow. Go to an exhibition of French Impressionists, very striking. Cocktail party for the Bishop of Croydon. Meet Dereck de Black, a young kilted New Zealander of Dutch extraction. Now both parents are in bed with flu. Dereck calls round with his black Alsatian, 'Senta', takes me to Hannover Zoo. We see gnus, emus, ostriches, alpacas, he takes a snap of me with my splint.

23rd February – Takes me to see *The Marriage of Figaro*, at the Operahaus. Superb! The costumes are brand-new, they were hidden under the stage during the war, and this is the first time they've been worn. I adore Mozart!

Thursday 24th February – Now *I'm* in bed with flu.

Friday 4th March – See the autobiographical play *The Corn is Green* by Emlyn Williams. Beatrix Lehman plays the school teacher who took him under her wing. It's excellent. Saturday, dinner at the Officers Club with the Wills, Griffiths, and Dereck de Black. We are later joined by the Paras and the airlift pilots. [The airlift to beleaguered Berlin had just begun.] See Major Willard, he's pleased with my progress. I'm having Short Waves and Ultra Violet Rays on my coccyx. CLOTHES RATIONING ENDS TODAY!

Go for a walk in the woods with Dereck. We see *The Secret Life of Walter Mitty*, very funny. Nan has altered her birth certificate, it might mean six months in jail! She did it because she was too young to get into the WRENS at the beginning of the war. She's in UK. Hope she'll be all right. Next day we hear she has been cleared, is going back into the WRENS as a Third Officer. My deltoid muscles have not regenerated, never will, also the left shoulder muscles, but they say other ones are trying to compensate – I must just try to build up muscle with lots of exercise, especially swimming.

Thursday 31st March – Nan arrives back, she's staying at the Central Hotel. I go to see *Die Zauberflote* (*The Magic Flute*) with Georgina. Superb singing, costumes, acting! Monday, train arrives with students from King Alfred's, how I miss school! With Dereck to the NAAFI and see Carol Reed's *Fallen Idol* – very good. Next day – choir practice, the Archbishop of York comes tomorrow.

Saturday 16th March – Clyde Fox, the Canadian from Prince Rupert's, and I go for a long walk to the Tiergarten (zoo), and back. We get on very well.

25th April – Go back to Detmold for a visit via Hamelin. Lovely old half-timbered black and white houses, very Pied Piperish! Narrow cobbled streets, positively medieval. See the Bredens and the Studemanns, everyone asks how I'm getting on. Dinner with Dr Thompson, nice. Back in Hannover, see *Scott of the Antarctic*, so sad. Saturday, go up to Bad Harzberg in the Harz Mountains, with Nan and Mummy. Stay in a ski resort with marvellous scenery. Climb up the Bergbaum, very thrilling. On the way down I see my old Scots orderly from Rinteln. I blush, thinking of him giving me that blanket bath.

26th April – Parents have changed their minds – I'm going back to school ... what made them change their minds? Have they come into money? Or is it the polio?

5th May – Back at school. It feels strange. They find me changed.

21st May – I lose my glasses. Sunday, I read the Lesson. Tuesday, am singing a solo. Everyone is tiptoeing around me, just because I'm wearing this bloody splint. We go to Hamburg to see *Hamlet*, with Laurence Olivier, in black and white. Wonderful!

1st June – 'A' for English. I've decided to take biology in School Cert. My arm has improved, the Doc says.

Sunday 5th June – Go out with Jane Arnot's parents, have a lovely time. (She's head girl, and we've become good friends.)

8th June – The choir goes to Hamburg to record for BFN (British Forces Network). Our voices sound pretty good.

9th June – The King's birthday. Trip to Scharbeutz cancelled. We go on a trip round our five lakes in a launch, which is more fun! Next day is Prince Phillip's birthday.

Tuesday 14th June – School Cert Exams start, I'm still writing with my right hand. I sing another solo, Greensleeves, Mummy's favourite. Millicheap sent Mervyn to ask if I will go to the pictures with him. Just because I stood up for him one day in class, he thinks I like him ... it was pity!

Wednesday 22nd June – There's a film company in the school. They're filming all aspects of KAS. I think it's to show people at home how we're mixing in with different nationalities. June Jago is in it, she has lovely curly brown hair with blonde highlights. Exams, have written English, History, Geography, Art. The latter I manage somehow by taking off my splint and holding my left hand. I can swim six lengths, and am jumping off the diving board. Letter from Nan, she's failed her driving test. Our play is off, I'm dreadfully disappointed. Our choir go to Prates to record. Peter Arnot asks me to have tea with him and his parents at Mill House, a beautiful old inn. Students from a Danish school come to stay, blonde, tanned, good-looking.

Letter from Pat. I see the Dr, he's thrilled with my progress, says I will be completely recovered within a year. I go with Jane to Hamburg to see the specialist. We look round the shops, go to the NAAFI. The devastation is so horrifying, flattened streets covered everywhere in greyish dust, only buildings like the cathedral rising starkly out of rubble. We usually go there at night to concerts etc, when the devastation doesn't show. As Jane says, London was bombed just as badly, and we didn't start the war. We treat ourselves to strawberries.

8th July – Millicheap asks me out again. I don't want to hurt his feelings, but he is so ugly, tall, thin, with a large beaky nose, and he has a sharp metallic smell ... I suppose it's nerves. He's totally misunderstood why I stood up for him – I don't like to see a person bullied, as I was for years when much younger.

Holidays: We go to a dance at the Yugoslav Embassy. Momcilovic is a sallow, overweight, but very pleasant boy in my class. His father is the Yugoslav Ambassador. They are celebrating Tito's birthday. All round the walls are banners with 'Long live Tito' on them (in Slav, of course). Mummy rigged up one of her old black cocktail dresses for me, I wanted to look sophisticated. A very dashing young Serb officer, shiny black knee-length boots, tight revealing jacket and breeches, with Mongolian slanted black eyes and devilish eyebrows, asks me to dance. He seems very excited, and whirls me around like a dervish. (I've ditched my splint for the evening.)

There is a really feverish atmosphere. Then a strange little hollow-cheeked man with pebble glasses asks me to dance. We pace sedately round the floor. He makes me feel nervous. Just for something to say I ask him what the banners say.

'Lonk live Tito. But let's not talk politics.' There was something very grim, even threatening about the way he said this. Later I danced with the Serb again. He warned me, 'Be careful what you say to that man, he is a Russian spy, with OGPU,' [this was before the KGB].

[The Cold War was getting worse, people talked about the 'Iron Curtain', and our pilots had to fly in supplies to the east side of Berlin because of the Berlin Wall. Now this may seem melodramatic, but my sister Nan was working for a secret operation, and we all knew things were very tense between the so-called Allies. The next day we heard that all the top members of the Embassy staff, including of course my school friend Momcilovic, had skipped over the border in the small hours while we were dancing, as did other Yugoslav loyalists all over Germany. Tito proclaimed himself independent of Russian overlordship! It was exciting to think we had helped to give them cover while they slipped away.]

Monday 29th August – My 17th birthday, it's Clyde Fox's 18th birthday as well so we have a joint small party in the evening. I can now discard my splint!

Wednesday 31st August – He takes me to the Caledonian Ball, we have a lovely time. Two bands, pipers, we dance lots of reels.

6th September – I have a driving lesson. We give a cocktail party, afterwards dine at the Chestnut Club with David Ramsden, Allen de Bray Faulkner, and Mack Mackinnon. Nan and Mack go to a dance together, Pat goes back to Bad Oeynhausen. (She's in the ATS, stationed there.)

24th September – David asks me to have dinner with him at the Tiergarten, ride back through the woods in his Jeep, very romantic!

Friday 16th September – Train back to school. 180 new children. Am now in the Upper Fifth, 6 boys and 6 girls. Reading *Lost Horizon* by James Hilton. Go for a long walk, and nearly tread on a hare. Weighed by the Dr, am 57 kg, height 5ft 5¾ ins. Pat Heriz-Smith is helping us to find a play. I swim, temperature 62.6. Cadets from HMS *Wrangler* play us at football, they also win the ping pong tournament against Temple Boys. Write to Rosemary Boswell, who was with me in hospital. Parcel from Mummy. My friend Tessa is in hospital. I'm feeling rotten. Write to Granpa in Scotland, and Clyde.

2nd October – A foxhunt. I sail in a pirate for the first time. Beautifully rough weather! Harvest Festival, sheaves of barley and fruit in church.

Friday 21st October – Go to Hamburg for a concert, Haydn Concerto for Trumpet and Orchestra. Saturday, meeting of the KABC Repertory Company (our grandiloquently titled radio network). I am to play Sylvia, in *Murder on the 2nd Floor*. Next day we see a waterspout on the lake while we travel around in a launch, celebrating King Alfred's birthday.

29th October – Halloween party, I wear a crinoline. While clearing up after the party next day I get a call from the parents and Nan, they travel back to UK tomorrow. Temple girls are gated for rowdiness!

5th November – Guy Fawkes day, I sell poppies. We have a huge bonfire and dress the guy in flags. There is an actual ring around the moon – eerie. Oberon bolted with me, not a pleasant ride! Letter from David. Paul Fillingham asks me to crew for him, great honour. I enjoy the sail, he is nicer than ever, has deep blue eyes and a well-bred voice. He plays the piano at assembly. My dorm has a midnight feast.

13th November – Broadcast of *Murder on the 2nd Floor*, it goes well.

Sunday 20th November – Cruise into next lakes with Carmel Hicks, and others. [Carmel was a delightful Canadian student, flashing smile, deep dimples, shiny brown hair, always dressed in kilts, sloppy tops and saddle shoes.]

Wednesday 23rd November – First exam of School Certificate – French Oral. I'm terribly nervous. The examiner has cross eyes, which is a little off-putting!

25th November – English Lit. not too bad, but I'm still writing with my right hand – hard. Hope they'll be able to read it. Geography, only do four out of five questions, run out of time. See Gerald about going home to UK.

28th November – English Language, quite nice. History, OK. Art, Pictorial Composition, and the next day, Life and object. Use my old painting for the Churchill competition for the Pictorial one, Patrick says it's all right as my arm isn't up to it.

8th December – Last exam, Biology. Thank God it's over!

13th December – Say goodbye to everybody, can hardly believe I'm really going home. A stormy passage on the North Sea, am very sick.

14th December – Arrive in Newcastle, we are in the same flat as three years ago. It's as though we've never been away. I develop flu, high temperature, probably stress of exams.

19th December– I start at the Newcastle Playhouse as an extra. *When Knights Were Bold* is a medieval spoof, quite funny. I've had flu with a high temperature, but didn't want to 'let the side down', so I rush to the theatre, put on my costume in a daze, and stagger on stage, having had to run past the battlements to get to the stage right … get an unintentional laugh, as my tall hennin headdress appears in mid air behind the crenellations (I was fixated on not disrupting the chain in the dance sequence). Not a good start to my career.

Reminds me of a story Patrick Heriz-Smith told us. He went to see a performance of *Tosca* in Italy, and after the tragic suicide leap over the castle walls, was surprised to see her ample body rebounding into the air beyond the castle walls! It must have been a very well-sprung mattress that she landed on.

Wednesday 21st December – Invited to the Evans' at Ridley Hall for a housewarming party. A lovely grey stone building, beautiful wild surroundings. It's good to see them all again. Meet their adopted daughter (Barbara). No one mentions my arm, which is a blessing. Very Christmassy, lots of cards on the huge mantelpiece. The log fire smoking a bit, green wood. Dik's eyes are red from the smoke, he's attentive, but I don't find him physically attractive. He has a tremendous sense of humour, however.

Diaries for approximately the next two years are missing. They were kept in an aluminium trunk, which was supposed to be waterproof. We put it on the verandah at Clarendon Heights in Bruce Street, and there was a fair amount of rain. Later I found out there was a tiny hole in the bottom and they were completely mouldy, so they had to be thrown away. As a result, dates can only be guessed at.

I did some more plays for Donald Gilbert's Playhouse during the two years, played Ethel in *Just William*, and appeared in *Family Affairs* and *Trespass*, with the haunting music by Phillip Addinsell. I was Mrs Miller, the Kathleen Harrison part, in an amateur production of *Flarepath*, a moving play about RAF pilots at the beginning of the war. I met Stella Garvey, a member of the Gateshead Socialist Party's Drama Group. They put on a stirring production of *The Recruiting Sergeant*, with her playing the protagonist like a principal boy, strangely enough it worked very well! Mummy disapproved of her of course, because she had a Geordie accent. She insisted I joined the Young Conservatives so as to meet the 'right people', so I went along to tennis parties, but my heart wasn't in it, I was far more of a socialist, in rebellion against the years of snobbery.

Mummy found me a job at 'Enid's', a tiny little shop in Osborne Road. It was owned by Mrs Marks, a stout overbearing Jewish woman who paid minimal wages. The window contained one garment, artfully accompanied by a pair of leather gloves, a fur stole maybe, and a hat. It was changed once a week. I learned how to stuff tissue paper

PLAYHOUSE NEWCASTLE

Chairman & Managing Director :
DONALD GILBERT.

Manager : VICTOR HILL.

3rd PROGRAMME

December 26th

When Knights Were Bold

A COMEDY, BY CHARLES MARLOWE

Characters :		
Sir Guy De Vere	---	BRUCE GORDON
Wittle	---	NORMAN RAEBURN
Barker	---	ROBERT KNIGHT
The Hon. Charles Widdicombe	---	RONALD DODA
Sir Bryan Ballymote	---	KENETH THORNETT
Mr. Isaac Isaacson	---	IVOR DEAN
Mr. Peter Pottleberry D.D.	---	CHARLES STAPLEY
Hawkins	---	PATRICK WALSH
Lady Rowena Waldegrove	---	RENEE CROOM
Mrs. Serena Eggington	---	DIANA JOHNS
Millicent Eggington	---	MARGARET DAVIS
Marjorie Eggington	---	STELLA GARVEY
Kate Pottleberry	---	FRIEDA GILLAT
Miss Isaacson	---	PATRICIA HAMILTON
Alice Barker	---	ANGELA NARRACOTT
		MARGARET MALLET
Court Ladies	---	SHIELA FERGUSON
		NANCY WINCH
		MONICA BELL
Soldiers	---	WILLIAM WAGGOTT
		WALTER PLINGE
Pages	---	ALAN ARMSTRONG
		DAVID GRAVELL

DONALD GILBERT

presents

"TRESPASS"

A Ghost Story by Emlyn Williams.

Music specially composed for the production by Richard Addinsell

Characters :		
Bill	---	RONALD WOOD
Gwen	---	PATRICIA HAMILTON
Maid	---	SHEILA FERGUSON
Mr. Once	---	KEITH WILLIAMS
Mrs. Henting	---	JESSICA NOAD
Christine	---	BARBARA INGRAM
Dewar	---	TERRY SOMMERVILLE
Mrs. Amos	---	MARGARET DAVISON
Saviello	---	IVOR DEAN
Philip Henting	---	

DONALD GILBERT presents

" JUST WILLIAM "

A Comedy by Alick Hayes

Based on the character "William" created by Richmal Crompton.

Characters :		
Magini the Magician	---	CHRISTOPHER BOND
William Brown	---	PETER McKENDRICK
Ginger	---	GORDON SPENCE
Violet Elizabeth Bott	---	ANNE KIRK
Egbert Huggins	---	MICHAEL ARRIS
Phyllis	---	JEAN HOLNESS
Ethel Brown	---	SHEILA FERGUSON
Mrs. Brown	---	BARBARA INGRAM
Robert Brown	---	RONALD WOOD
Mr. Brown	---	CHARLES STAPLEY
Miss Milton	---	BARBARA WILSON
Dulcie	---	PATRICIA HAMILTON
Uncle Noel	---	ROGER TRAFFORD
First Fireman	---	ROBERT KNIGHT
Second Fireman	---	FREDERICK CABLE
Peter Slade	---	ROBERT WEEDEN
Bill Hargreaves	---	CHRISTOPHER BOND
Inspector White, C.I.D.	---	DAVID BROWN
Det. Sgt. Smith, C.I.D.	---	FREDERICK CABLE
Sergeant	---	ROBERT KNIGHT
		MARGERY SCOTT
		CARYL WEARS
		RAIE BREWIS

DONALD GILBERT

presents

FAMILY AFFAIRS

A Comedy by Gertrude Jennings.

Characters :		
Lady Madehurst	---	BARBARA INGRAM
Sidney	---	IVOR DEAN
Herbert } her sons	---	TERRY SOMMERVILLE
Harvey	---	CHRISTOPHER BOND
Sarah, her daughter	---	JESSICA NOAD
Amy Wigmore, her sister	---	ELIZABETH KELL
Nevil, her grandson	---	RONALD WOOD
Mrs. Herbert Madehurst, Julia	---	BARBARA WILSON
Mrs. Nevil Madehurst, Rose	---	PAMELA WRIGHT
Margaret Hamilton	---	SHEILA FERGUSON
Helena Warwick	---	PAMELA BROUGHTON
Hannah	---	OLIVE WR

My early cast listings

in the curves and twist the tiny waist, nothing so obvious as a mannequin, it was all such good taste! Mrs Redgrave was the manageress, she was sweet, amply covered, with fat ankles and a lush mouth revealing plenty of gums when she smiled. She had a tiny snuffly Pekinese. If a man came into the shop (ahem, boutique), she would surge towards him in an outrageously flirtatious manner.

They didn't know about my gammy arm, which was fine, but sometimes I wished they wouldn't ask me to lift and rearrange heavy fur coats and boxes. I flourished a feather duster in the best stage maid's manner, and found out how to fold and pack carefully with aforesaid tissue paper. The clothes were good quality – the clientele, middle to upper.

1950

The results of the School Certificate Exam arrived. I had Distinctions in art and English literature, Credits in English language, biology, history, geography, and French. Not having taken maths I couldn't qualify for Matric, but could at least claim Matric Standard. Don't know how they read my writing. I applied to Newcastle Education Authority for a bursary to RADA.

Mack Mackinnon of the Royal Signals, Nan's old boyfriend, called a few times. She had met her husband-to-be, Major Colin Pringle, and was engaged, so Mack very sweetly started asking me out. He was all of 28, ancient in my eyes, but he was a thoroughly nice man, and never tried to overstep the mark. I went to Catterick and stayed in a hotel near the camp, in Richmond, Yorkshire. He smoked a pipe, and drove me all over Yorkshire in his old Rover. He took me to a performance of *Our Town* by Thornton Wilder. The Arena Theatre Group were touring with a new concept – theatre in the round, the audience being seated around the stage. It was new to the fifties, but would have been familiar to Shakespeare's Globe audiences.

Our Town was perfect for this kind of staging, as it was set in an imaginary town, with few props, imaginative lighting, and some changes of level. Next time I saw *Candida* by Bernard Shaw. A very different kettle of fish! Typical Edwardian setting – furniture and props everywhere, difficult to stage so that all the audience could see. It was far more suitable for a normal proscenium arch stage. They were brave to attempt it. Seeing these plays fired my ambition to go to RADA. I had written to request an audition, and there were some nail-biting weeks waiting for the answer.

Anders von Buchwald wrote to me from Denmark, but the unlikelihood of seeing him again soon made writing to him a bit of a chore. David Ranft, the signals officer I had met in Germany, wrote to me from Singapore, enclosing marvellous cards embellished with shavings of cork to form fantastic landscapes, scented with sandalwood.

Dik Evans wrote from the RAF training camp at Calne, where he was doing his National Service. His letters were virtually unreadable, but I could tell he had a sweetly comical outlook.

Bill Eldon resurfaced; he had taken Nan out before we went to Germany. Now I was nubile 17 he asked me out to dinner. I was terribly nervous, he was very quiet. He drove me to a restaurant on the cliffs near Whitley Bay. You took a lift down to just above sea level, and sat watching the spray dashing against the windows. It was an Italian style place; I chose lobster thermidor, which was delicious. He plied me with chianti and got me talking about life in Germany, then, as the tide was going out, suggested we walk along the sand. I demurred; I'd ruin my new, thin, high-heeled sandals and stockings. 'Take 'em off,' he hinted.

So we traipsed along, my shoes and stockings dangling from one hand, the other tucked under his arm. Then he stopped, turned to me and began kissing me with great expertise. Open mouth kisses were new to me. 'I've wanted to kiss you ever since I first saw you,' he muttered, as we paused for breath, 'but I thought you didn't like me.' I said, 'You looked so bored.' He answered that with increasingly passionate kisses, his other hand touching my breasts. I began to feel threatened and begged him to take me home. I was still a virgin and intended to remain that way for a long time, I believed in the old-fashioned idea of staying 'pure' until marriage. At the garden gate he kissed me goodnight, but then he said he couldn't bear to say goodbye, swept me into his arms, and we started walking aimlessly, ending up in Jesmond Dene, a sort of lover's lane, on a bench, kissing and murmuring sweet nothings for hours.

Bill went away to Bart's (St Bartholomews) medical school in London and I didn't see him for some months. He did write, but his letters were curiously stilted and uninformative. After a while I began to wonder if that evening really happened. In the meantime I'd been to stay with Dik and his family at Ridley a few times, and had grown fond of them all. Freda had returned from her secret war work, and I got to know and admire her. She, like Eryk, had a wonderful sense of humour, and a strong Christian faith, which never obtruded or became prosy. We often played charades, which was quite a craze in the pre-TV years. They were not card players, as so many families were, but would rather read and listen to music. I felt more at home with them than with my own hostile blood relatives.

Dik's letters were completely unlike Bill's:

Dearest Sheila, (or may I call you Miss Ferguson?)
Far away from your distraction, and in the chilly light of a Yorkshire day, I feel more able to appreciate your mournful departure. Just because of some suddenly arisen – though doubtless truly loved and lasting star – you have left me, apparently resolved not to see me again, or some such nonsense. Perhaps it does not occur to you that it is quite possible to know me and continue 'La Grande Passion' in Newcastle at the same time ... or is your much sought after heart incapable of such a strain? It seems a little pointless to me – but then I am biased, being the bereft one. Perhaps your favourite flower [Sweet William – Bill Eldon] might not approve of my meeting you in Newcastle, but perhaps he will permit a few innocent and deckle-edged letters from you to lighten the lead-lined chunk of stone that I pass off as my heart. Forgive my bitterness, I can't keep up being stoical for very long, I miss you far too much for comfort,
Yours, Dik.

P.S. Margot Fonteyn has consented to grace my locker door, she was far too big to fit into my scrap book. She rivals coloured hussies from Blighty and Razzle. I must apologise for the shortcomings of Ridley Hall. I mended 2 lights that apparently left you in darkness and I hear you were cold in the night; that, combined with my agonized pleadings – must have all conspired against my suit. I hope they won't prevent you coming back again, would love to have you stay, third time lucky. Love Dik.

My father found a job as a representative of an engineering company, and was away from home quite a lot, which should have pleased my mother. She still followed the same routine as before we left for Germany, shopping, coffees with Elsie; it never occurred to her to find a job or an interest in life. Now she was accusing him of having affairs with women while away, and he probably did, but at least he never left us in the lurch, always provided for us, so in that sense he was a good father. I was in a kind of limbo, waiting to hear from RADA, waiting to hear from the education people about my bursary. Working at Enid's helped to fill up the days, but Mrs Marks's petty spiteful meanness hardly made the pittance I earned at all worthwhile.

Billy Metcalfe was an amiable young man, and he took me out to the odd film. My mother insisted I go out with other people, she thought Bill was to old for me, and in those days one tended to go out with a variety of boys and flirting was considered normal. Billy was a typical Geordie, tall, thin, with a wide engaging smile. He'd gone to a good school, and his family were well-to-do, so Mummy approved of him. If she'd known what he got up to ... He took me to the Hoppings on the Town Moor. This was a kind of annual fair, with coconut shies, airgun stalls, Test your Weight machines, fortune tellers with glass balls and gypsy earrings. He won a kewpie doll, we had sticky drinks, then wandered off to the pond. I used to sail boats on the pond, but by this time the boats were remote controlled, usually by elderly men.

We were lying on the grass indulging in what was known as petting, when a flashlight shone on us – it was a policeman. He told us to move on. That part of the moor was regularly used by lovers who, without a car, had nowhere to go and no privacy at home. In daylight after the fair you would see FLs as they were known (condoms), scattered all over the place. Pregnancy was a constant fear, there was no Pill, and no AIDS of course. The Odeon cinema was the other refuge. Red velvet tip-up seats, close together, the back seats full of writhing youngsters (who had not yet been labelled teenagers). In the interval the grinning, bobbing organist who rose from the depths in front of the screen, in his white tuxedo, was my bête noir. The lights would go on and the audience would be shown up in all their disarray. The music was awful too, jazzed-up versions of popular songs. Elderly usherettes in unflattering short frilly skirts would wander round with trays of cigarettes, chocolates and ice creams. I considered snogging in the back row to be vulgar, besides someone might see me and report back to Mummy! Yes, smoking was allowed, hard to believe now, and in theatres and cinemas healthy lungs were exposed to passive and active smoking. I'd started to smoke the occasional cigarette, but not in front of the parents, it was an attempt to appear sophisticated and I didn't really enjoy it.

The heroes, back from the war, were just coal miners again, back to short pay, no bathrooms in the slum back-to-back houses, taking refuge in the pub on Fridays, wife and kids huddled outside with a bag of chips if they were lucky. There were pithead baths, but they could never get rid of that ingrained blackness. Still, there was a great feeling of optimism in the air, the middle classes were better off than before the war, and the Labour government was in power.

At last the letter came – my appointment to audition. By this time Pat was living in London, working in the Personnel Training Department of Harrods, and staying at Helen Graham House, opposite the British Museum. I could stay with her. Helen Graham House was the head of the YWCA organisation. I went down by train, so nervous I had awful collywobbles. We had to prepare a speech by Mary Queen of Scots, which starts, 'I am lost, Beaton...' The emphasis was unclear: did it mean she was lost, *beaten* as in defeated? Or did it mean *Beaton*, her Lady-in Waiting? I decided it only made sense if she was speaking to the latter. I know some of the hopefuls had misunderstood and put in the wrong emphasis, so it was a trick test in a way. I had no one to coach me with the pieces: the other was a speech by Rosalind from *As You Like It* and one I had to choose myself, I think it was a speech by Emily from *Our Town*. I was terribly green, but they could tell I had sincerity and strong feeling. I had my mother to thank for the fact that I didn't have a Geordie accent.

The bursary came through, and RADA wrote to say I was too immature to join straight away, but I could enrol at PARADA (Preparatory Academy), in Highgate, North London. I was over the moon! I left Newcastle and Enid's, full of excitement. I shared a bedroom with Pat and her friend Mary Lynch at Helen Graham, and travelled on the Northern Line to Highgate every day. I found out Karl Marx was buried in the cemetery nearby: I was in rarified company. Even more amazing was the fact that my old dancing partner, Charles Ross, was in his last term there, and his sidekick, Sam, from the Guards, also! They were a lot older than us 18-year-olds.

Pat was going out with Clive Montague Brooks. They had met

Ridley Hall, Dik's home

The elfin cut!

My first publicity photo

while doing in a play together in BAOR. Now he was in a play at the Whitehall Theatre, *Reluctant Heroes*, with Brian Rix.

We had both found the hours at Helen Graham House a bit restrictive, especially as Clive finished his stint at the theatre rather late, and she was supposed to be in by 10.30. Quite often we had to creep in via a window that had been left open by our friends, it was like being back at school. So we found a flatlet in Swiss Cottage, convenient for me as it was on the Northern Line. It was a top floor, dormer-windowed two-room flat, sharing the bathroom with another lodger, and in my room there was a cupboard with a two-ring gas plate. It was just as well I had been to boarding school and was used to keeping my cubicle tidy! Pat piled her clothes onto an armchair in her room, and only put them away when they toppled over from sheer gravity. There was wardrobe in her room, but I had to hang my clothes from the picture rail. Our landlord was a kindly German Jewish doctor, who didn't mind what time we came in at night as long as we were quiet.

I went to book a return train ticket home to Newcastle on my first vac. It was evening and I was in a gloomy mood, not looking forward to a renewal of exposure to the inevitable and bitter warfare between my parents. I caught the eye of a man sitting in front of me. He was looking at me in the reflection of the window. He smiled. Normally I would have ignored an obvious come-on, but the rebellious mood inspired me to think, 'What the hell!' I smiled back. He got off the bus at the same stop as me and greeted me:

'You look sad, lady, what is wrong?' He was a foreigner, Spanish-looking. We started chatting and he waited while I went to the ticket office. His English was pretty bad so, foolishly, I felt no sense of a threat, just a lonely guy who'd recently arrived in UK and knew no one... He said he liked opera, and there was a film, *Lucia di Lammermoor*, would I like to go with him? I had nothing planned for the rest of the evening so I agreed to go.

In the cinema his hot hand and garlicky mouth began to explore, and I kept turning my mouth away and swatting his hand, but he would persist, getting bolder each time. The film was awful, in Italian with no subtitles, and I began to wonder how to get away from him. We were in the middle of a row, so I couldn't just leap up and make a run for it. I had a bright idea, why not suggest going for a walk afterwards, then I could get away easily. We walked in St James Park and he pulled me down onto a bench, and began fumbling with his flies, while clinging onto me with his other hand – it was now or never. As he pulled out the object of the exercise I scarpered! I ran wildly, not knowing which direction to go, with him shouting at me to come back. Memories of dreadful tales of what can happen to young girls in London, white slavery, Jack the Ripper, swirled in my brain.

I saw a gate and ran to it, shouting, 'Help!' A sentry on duty at St James Palace spotted me and opened the gate enough to let me slip in. My Spaniard rattled at the gate and swore in remarkably fluent English. He was told to 'Hop it!' They were so kind, could see I was in shock and gave me a cup of tea and a biscuit. I explained what had happened and my sentry told me off for taking such a chance. I was put in a taxi, they paid for it as I couldn't afford it, and I arrived back in Swiss Cottage in style. I never told Pat, she would have been furious with me, but it was a good lesson, and I was very lucky to escape.

The Principal of PARADA was Eric Capon, an avuncular man who encouraged his students and gave us the confidence in ourselves that was the main ingredient lacking. Not in Charles Ross, however. He and Sam were in their twenties, sophisticated men-about-town. He and I started a little dalliance, but he wanted to cut to the chase, and I wasn't prepared to jettison my principles just for a casual fling. He had changed, those blue eyes were cynical, he'd become hard, there was no spark, and I longed for Bill Eldon.

Charles later met Elizabeth Wallace, a lovely dark-haired Scots girl who studied with me at RADA, and married her. He became a theatrical impresario. Joe Orton and Kenneth Halliwell were in my class. Joe was a thin, gangly boy with a wide cheeky grin, and an outrageous sense of humour. Kenneth was different, short, plump, with pouchy eyes, but he had a very good voice. He also had the camp mannerisms that betrayed his sexual orientation. I had never come across gays before. I'd read about Oscar Wilde, of course, but it was a different matter to be in close proximity with them. We got on very well; I found them to be intelligent and sensitive.

Wilfred Walter, a marvellous old actor who taught us Radio Technique, put Kenneth and me up for a piece on the Alfred Marks Show for the BBC. Two students were selected from the main drama schools and given a scene from certain modern dramatists to prepare. We did an excerpt from Jean Anouilh's *Antigone*, the moving scene where she has been entombed in a cave and she talks to the soldier guarding her. Afterwards, Wilfred wrote us a lovely letter saying he thought we did well, and were as good as any of the other students who had preceded us. We became friends, and we visited him in hospital subsequently. He told the most amusing anecdotes, and resembled Merlin with his flowing white hair and beard.

At the end of the first term I played Hermione in *A Winter's Tale*. Eric Capon said in his report, 'I was most impressed by her performance at the end of term, and am convinced she has real talent.' The next term was spring 1951, and he gave me a good report, so I was then considered mature enough to move to RADA proper in Gower Street.

1951

Miss Brown was the secretary, and the first person one met on arrival. She had buck teeth and wispy hair dragged into an untidy bun. I swear she hated the students. We learned fencing with Mr Froeschlen, who had a huge white moustache. I enjoyed fencing very much but it was hard, because my arm would start to sag. No one knew I'd had polio, so I had to somehow disguise the weakness. Dancing was known as Movement and the class was run by a stick-thin Swedish lady. It was all about 'filling space', and intended to relax the uptight English reserve. Voice Production was run by Miss Olive King, she had a sonorous deep voice, wore her black hair in a tight bun, and was elegantly turned out in power suits. I had problems with projection from the start, my lungs just didn't put out enough sound.

The first term we performed *Pink String and Sealing Wax*, produced by Juliet Mansel. I played the mother, Mrs Strachan. Ernest Hall produced *As You Like It*, I played Rosalind. He told me I must get more experience. I was supposed to kiss my father, Duke Orsino, played by Stan Thomasson, an American. I stuck my bottom out, so he told me to get closer to the Duke ... in fact, he asked me if I'd ever kissed my own father. It was a sore point, since I hated him. Afterwards we had a little chat and, in a delicate way, he hinted that I needed to get sexual experience if I wanted to be any kind of actress. I was taken aback – what about 'remaining a virgin till I married'?

John and I were good friends, and we'd both come up from PARADA. I suggested that we needed this mythical experience, so let's try it. Well – it was the funniest afternoon ... more like an anatomy class, and we couldn't stop laughing! We agreed to remain platonic friends since he couldn't get it up. I began to realise that love had to enter into the equation somewhere, or at least strong physical attraction. Bill Eldon had phoned me in Newcastle and suggested we meet in London, so maybe I should do something about meeting him again. I was afraid to spoil the unearthly promise of that first date.

Bill had digs in Clapham Common. Instead of meeting me and taking me out to dinner, as I expected, he gave me directions how to get there. It was quite a trek from Swiss Cottage. On arrival at the dingy lodgings he gave me a beer, and a book on forensic medicine full of horrific photos of raped and dead vaginas! Meanwhile he cooked us steak on a gas ring – the meat was very tough. Then he led me through to his bedroom and clumsily tried to take me by force. I refused to remove my jersey, but he pulled off my slacks and just went in without foreplay. He didn't use a condom. He hurt me inside and I yelped in pain.

'You're not a virgin!' he said triumphantly, 'You said you were!' He thought he knew it all, being a medical student – maybe anatomically he did (but that brute would never make a good doctor, only a butchering surgeon). I knew that I had been a virgin before he interfered with me, and was one no longer, but I wasn't going to argue the toss. I struggled back into my clothes and ran out of that sordid place.

If they had found out, my parents would have said I was foolish to go to his digs alone, to trust him at all, asking for trouble. So it was really my fault. Nowadays we would call what happened date rape. With hindsight I suppose it tickled his vanity to think it was the first time for me, but there were no real feelings of affection, even of enjoyment of the act. For weeks I was apprehensive in case I was pregnant, but thank God I wasn't. I never heard from him again. On reflection, I assumed it must have been that bumpy ride on the bony back of the potato carthorse that had effectively ripped my hymen.

Joan Collins was in her final year when I entered RADA. She was very lovely: huge brown eyes, tiny waist, her hair wasn't thick, it was fine like mine. She was the daughter of Nat Collins, the music hall agent. She was going out with Gabriel Woolf – he was a dish, tall, with curly blond hair. Everyone said she wasn't much of an actress, but soon after she left she had parts in films, so she was good enough for that! Diane Cilento shimmied across the stage in a bikini, in a non-speaking role, at the Final Show, and the following day was deluged in offers by producers and agents...

Margaret Whiting was in another set but the same term as I. She had been acting with the Bristol Old Vic for two years. Her voice was deep and carrying, and she looked about 35 although reputedly only 18. We were all in awe of her experience. Graham Armitage was also in her set. He was an ordinary lad from a working class home, although his father was a vicar. He was very camp in his mannerisms, an amusing person. Jimmy Whitely gave great parties, he was in the same clique as Charles and Sam. I went out with him once or twice. Sue Holman, Vivien Leigh's daughter, had big blue eyes and short curly hair. She was no great actress, but was a lovely, funny friend.

I began to wonder if I had the necessary staying power to achieve success as an actress. I really battled to produce enough volume and projection on stage, and we were constantly warned how little work there was 'out there'. I had no desire to be a 'star' as such, I wanted to model myself on actors like Alec Guinness, who submerged himself in the character, unlike Laurence Olivier whose characters were always parts of himself. I would have loved to have gone to university, to study history, literature, or archaeology, but without maths there was no chance. Then I would remember that my parents were making sacrifices to keep me at college, and I'd better keep my nose to the grindstone!

1952

Some of the other plays we did in the next few terms were *Wild Decembers* by Clemence Dane (I played Charlotte); *Iphigenia in Aulis* (Iphigenia); *The Women Have Their Way* by Lorca (Santita); *Random Harvest* by James Hilton (Lydia); *The Duchess of Malfi* by Webster (the Duchess); *Venus Observed* by Christopher Fry (Lydia); *Pillars of Society* by Ibsen (Mrs Bernick). I was Nicole in *Le Bourgeois Gentilhomme* by Moliere, and Autolycos in *The Winter's Tale*. Unfortunately I caught a bad cold, and was afraid I'd miss the performance. Hanna Nowatska, a fat Polish student who was playing Autolycos in the other cast, phoned me and suggested I got out of bed and went for a brisk walk. I struggled out of bed and went for a long walk to the top of Hampstead. There I fainted, and the next thing I knew I was in hospital with pleurisy! She must have done a voodoo spell on me ... so I missed the actual performance anyway.

We all used to eat at Ollivelli's – it was just round the corner, and did a fine spaghetti bolognese for only one and ninepence. At parties everyone brought bottles of cheap red wine, barsac, or chianti. Hemingway was all the rage, you just weren't in the swim if you didn't have at least one poster of a bullfighter on the wall, and you scored extra brownie points if you had a leather wine bottle from Spain hanging around somewhere. Most of us were living on next to nothing.

But we did get comps (complimentary tickets), for all the plays on in the West End, which was marvellous. I saw *Ring Around the Moon* by Anouilh, with Claire Bloom and Dirk Bogarde, their first big parts, and they were superb. I also saw *Colombe*, again by Anouilh (he was definitely flavour of the year), with Yvonne Arnaud. The craze for anything French extended to cinema: la nouvelle vague. Two new plush movie houses opened, with seats that didn't tip up but were like armchairs: the Berkely and Carlton. There we saw *Orphée* with Jean Marais, *Les Enfants du Paradis* with Jean-Louis Barrault, *Sous les Toits de Paris*, a very surreal film, *La Ronde* with Anton

Walbrook, *Casque d'Or* with a glorious Simone Signoret, and various films by Jean Cocteau. I wanted to study at the Sorbonne once I left the Academy.

Ronald Harwood, a friend of mine, was carrying a spear at the Lyric, Hammersmith and gave me tickets. This was Donald Wolfit's company. I saw him in *King Lear* and he was magnificent. Nowadays people dismiss him when compared with, say, Olivier, but he was a good actor. Unfortunately he surrounded himself with bad actors, in the mistaken conviction that it would make his acting look better ... he cast his wife Rosalind Iden as Cordelia, and she wore long flaxen plaits reminiscent of a Valkyrie or Brunhilde, I think she was in her fifties. She also played Juliet. (In the old days of fit-up rep, older actresses tended to play all the juicy parts, even if they were too old, and no one really complained.) The critics were not at all impressed.

Alec Guinness played in a modern dress *Hamlet*, which I found very moving. Another fine performance was Alec Clunes (Martin's father), as Richard II. I saw wonderful Pamela Brown and John Gielgud in *The Lady's Not for Burning* by Christopher Fry (playing a small part was Richard Burton). Fry had several plays going and was very popular, another was *A Phoenix Too Frequent.* His were verse plays, something new, a real break with the tradition of drawing-room comedies in stiff-upper-lip prose, à la Terence Rattigan and Noel Coward. T.S Eliot's *A Cocktail Party* was another blank verse play, which had a star-studded cast.

Some diaries did survive the damp trunk that year:

Tuesday 1st January – It snows. Go to BBC in Newcastle to arrange for an audition in London.

Monday 7th January – Dik comes over, bringing a black kitten, half Siamese. We name him Oscar.

Monday 26th January – Go to 100 Oxford Street – the Jazz Club with Richard T. Dance to Humphrey Lyttleton's Band. It's a tiny little square, heel toe style to trad jazz.

Wednesday 6th February – The King dies, great mourning everywhere.

He was so much loved, he and the Queen were very brave during the Blitz, mingling with the bereaved in the ruins of the East End. They said they were glad Buckingham Palace had been bombed, as it made them share in the common suffering of their people.

Friday 8th February – Dinner with Eric Steinberg, a friend of Dik's. Dik is now at Christ's College, Cambridge.

Monday 11th February – Go to the 'Prospect of Whitby' pub at Wapping with Terry Bayler. It's a favourite hang out with the younger set, it's as old as Shakespeare's Globe Theatre, and the ceiling is hung with weird mementos. Terry is a charming boy from our same term, a tall dark-skinned New Zealander, with black curly hair and a great sense of humour. Later we watch the procession of the King's coffin to Westminster Abbey, he'll lie in state there till Friday.

Thursday 14th February – See *Colombe* with Terry, very good. He comes back to my place. Pat isn't there...

Friday 15th February – Funeral of His Majesty, but we miss it, we don't get up in time. I adore him! He takes me to Regent's Park, see *A Midsummer Night's Dream* with Robert Atkins as Bottom.

Saturday 16th February – Pat, Clive, Terry and I go on a small pub crawl. Start off at the Swiss Cottage pub, then on to the 'Spaniards' on the Heath, all brown and smoky, with a mad talking parrot! We talk of ghosts ... afterwards walk back on the Heath in a really spooky mist!

Saturday 23rd February – Go to Arts Theatre with Terry, Kerry Jordan [another New Zealander in Terry's set] and Kaysa, a tall, blonde, Swedish girl who did the 'Snow Goose' for her audition piece, and when she reprised it in class went up on her high-booted toes as if flying – strangely comical!

29th February – Leap year, Daddy's birthday. They have moved down from Newcastle and live in a flat with large bow windows and a nice balcony, 135 Haverstock Hill. Terry and I have a mad shopping expedition at Harrods to find him a birthday present.

Saturday 1st March – Party at Jimmy Whiteley's, bring a bottle, super party. Nan and Colin came to see us but I missed them.

10th March – Go to stay with Nan and Colin in Salisbury, to recover from pleurisy. [Diaries for April to June 1952 are missing.]

Saturday 8th July – Go to Café de Paris, join the Guinea Pig Club there. See Noel Coward. What a joy – suave, polished performance, brilliant evening. To 'over egg the pudding', Marlene Dietrich is on after him! She wears a magnificent see-through gown, peach-coloured, sparkling with brilliants. I look for the zip – but can't spot it. People say it's a fine rubber garment which she pulls on over her old wrinkly body! Anyhow she is in fine voice, simply wonderful, and still very alluring and slim.

Monday 21st to Thursday 24th July – Verse Competition. C. Day Lewis one of the judges. Also V C Clinton Baddeley, who said I had a 'truly musical voice' and Patric Dickinson said 'excellent reading'.

16th August – Pat and Clive get married. New address 51 Greencroft Gardens. NW6. I get a card from Dik who's in Greece. Finish reading Gilles de Rais, Kafka's diaries.

Saturday 18th October – BBC, 2.30–5.30. Desmond Walter Ellis Show.

Thursday 23rd October – We do *Random Harvest.* Jack Salamanca is so miscast. He plays a truly English man and he has this Texan drawl, and always wears high-heeled cowboy boots. He is Indian dark, as is his wife Mimi, she has broad high cheekbones, a typical 'Mother Earth'. I play Kenneth Halliwell's wife, Jack's sister-in-law.

15th November – Brian Rawlinson's 21st birthday party, held at Jack's flat, 42A Linden Gardens, W2. Lovely home, full of bright Mexican wall hangings. [Years later Jack wrote *Lilith*, which sold well, and was made into a film.] I meet Laurence, a blond businessman type, mad about actors. He takes me out to Skindles, a popular restaurant beside the Thames near Henley.

17th November – Go to see *Porgy and Bess* by Gershwin. All Negro cast, brilliant! Wonderful singing, especially Cab Calloway, in 'It Ain't Necessarily So', he brings the house down! 'Summertime', so moving I cried.

Tuesday 18th November – Preliminaries for the Bossom and Tree Competitions, I'm selected for the Tree.

Friday 21st November – Tree Competition. I do Queen Catherine from Henry VIII. Sir Kenneth recalls three of us to repeat our performances because they can't decide who was the best. I had put so much into it initially, I had 'shot my bolt' and didn't have the strength or technique to do it again with the same intensity. [Margaret Whiting won, of course: she produced the identical emotion, using the technique honed during her 2 years at the Bristol Old Vic. I don't remember who the third girl was. Margaret went on to play Cleopatra at Stratford in 1953, so I guess I did quite well.] As a consolation I won the Hannam-Clarke Dialect Competition, and received the princely sum of 4 guineas!

Monday 24th November – Bossom Competition. Mime plays, and a potted version of the Globe Revue. Tuesday, audition for photos for *Country Life* magazine.

Friday 28th November – Navy League Ball, very posh, at the Festival Hall. I think I went with John Impey, one of the army guys I'd met when staying with Nan and Colin. Band of the Royal Marines, Hornpipe and Flamborough Sword Dance by Sea Cadets, and amazingly, good old Burl Ives, big and gorgeous, he was billed as 'The Wayfaring Stranger'! I wore a strapless white satin and net creation, in an Edwardian style with a bustle.

Wednesday 3rd December – Shoot *Country Life* photos. Tests for

Kendall Competition. Go to see *Quadrille* with Dik. [He used to pop in and out of my life, taking me to the odd film or play when he happened to be in town.]

Saturday 6th December – Dinner with David [the Signals officer I'd known in Germany. His father was a bank manager in Tunbridge Wells.] A very laid back American from the deep South, whose idea of heaven was sitting on top of a hill having his back scratched by a beautiful woman, took us out to meet some West Point cadet friends of his. They wore their grey spiffy uniforms and they were out for fun! We went to various pubs and nightspots, and ended up in their hotel room drinking bourbon out of the big round white light fittings (as they had no glasses).

1953

30th May – Tennis Club. [I was never much good at tennis, partly because of lack of strength in my left arm, but also because I had no eye for a ball.] Enjoy it very much. Allied Circle. [This was a good excuse for a party. Loved speaking French. Used to dress up in a black cocktail frock, usually one of my mother's cut down to fit me, and wear a little black hat with a bit of veiling. Drink wine, or gin and it, or gin and orange, eat tiny sausages on sticks, and smoke, preferably sporting a long cigarette holder. This way you never needed to talk to anyone as all your wits were involved in juggling these various accoutrements! Then a kind gentleman would often come to your aid to relieve you of one or other of the items.]

Tuesday 2nd June – Coronation of Queen Elizabeth II. We view the procession from the balcony of the Whitehall Theatre (Clive was acting in *Reluctant Heroes* there.) She looks absolutely fairy-like, perfect peachy skin, blue eyes. Philip looks even better, tall, with thick blond hair. Then we watch the actual ceremony in the Abbey on TV. The crown looks so heavy above the solemn little face, and the robes, encrusted with precious gems, seem to weigh her down. She has such dignity. [A rumour went around afterwards that she was wearing a rubber bag, because she would not have been able to pee for several hours … she must have been so nervous, but she had such willpower, maybe the bag wasn't necessary!] Clive is supposed to be the illegitimate son of the actor Clive Brook – who knows? We watch a wonderful firework display from Chelsea Bridge.

Friday 5th June – Meet John O'Brian at the New Lindsay Theatre in Notting Hill Gate about a part. He's a tall red-haired Irishman, but with no accent. I don't get the part, but he invites me to a party in Hampstead. [Later in the year he invited me to several more parties, where I met Gordon Price, Tony Payne and, eventually, Peter Blandy.] I meet Jeremy there. He's a printer, and is busy writing a novel. [We started going out together. I read some pages of his novel and found it very boring.]

Monday 8th June – Dik asks me to the May Ball at Christ's College, Cambridge. Have a lovely time! [Next morning we were still at it, wearing somewhat bedraggled gowns, eating strawberries and cream, being poled along in punts by dishevelled Hugh Grant lookalikes.]

Warring Clouds – Cambridge (with Dik Evans at May Ball)
Written at Murray Hutchins, 1954

Above our heads swing wild high
Cloud towers swooping 'bout the moon,
Pale and wan with care
Encircled by angry skeins
That harry and pursue
Bellying across her face
Clutching with frenzied fingers...
Yet has the moon an ample calm
'Midst her retinue of warring vapours.

As if to join that bright conflict
Bells and chimes well out around
Paeans of reassuring joy,
The steeples seem to tilt and sway
In ecstasy, silvered walls agleam
Against night's blue-black shield,
Now tired thoughts blow up and up...
They vanish whirling with
Her cloud-knight's charge...

Wednesday 17th June – See Gian-Carlo Menotti's opera, *The Medium*, with John Impey. Wonderful!

Thursday 18th June – Prizegiving at RADA. I am awarded a Diploma. Sir Kenneth presents me with the RADA Keepsake and Counsellor.

Athene Seyler gives a speech about not expecting too much when we get out into the wide world. We are all in a daze of excitement.

Friday 19th June – Photo session with John Brown. I bring white evening dress, roses, stage make-up. [These were my official stage photos to go into *Spotlight*, the actor's directory, essential for work.]

ROYAL ACADEMY OF DRAMATIC ART
62-64, GOWER STREET, LONDON, W.C.1

STUDENT'S REPORT   *Spring*   TERM 1953

NAME FERGUSON. Sheila   *Finals* I. DIVISION

VOICE PRODUCTION: *Sheila's voice is not naturally strong... I urge her to keep up her vocal technique especially the use of deep well controlled breathing. Vigorous effective tongue movement & to avoid tension... "Purity" so that she may make the best use of her utterance. I wish her well.* C.

Signed

DICTION:

Signed

ACTING - *the Arbitration.*

Sheila has deep feel. but her work is still lightweight & lacks strength. She is full of interest & a very good emotional actress - if she could develop physically she should do very well. Ruth Robinson

Rather uncertain of herself Sheila have really settled down in the role of Portia in 'Commedia-al-Law'. It is so excellent & effective - but that I find it difficult to understand why Sheila did not 'take hold' of the ...

Signed

PRINCIPAL'S REMARKS

An excellent student - Her Course has been characterised by steady progress. Her acting has the quality of sincerity; she must acquire a fuller and more elegance sense of emotional expression with the experience on the Stage, which she deserves, & I hope she will get. She has been awarded a Diploma K. Barnes

Next term begins ———— The Principal must be notified (in the case of provisional notice having been given) by ———— definitely whether the student is returning or not; failing the receipt of notification, the full fees for next term will be payable.

My final report from RADA

Saturday 20th June – Spend the weekend with John Impey at his parents' stately home. Most enjoyable. [His mother wore pearls and dung-coloured twinsets and skirts, I wore black, she did not approve of me. He was a typical 'deb's delight', they were wealthy, and she did not intend him to marry a penniless actress!]

Monday 22nd June – RADA dance. Say goodbye to most of my friends.

Tuesday 23rd June – Studio 5 for model photos. Take evening frock, hat, suit, brolly, gloves.

Wednesday 24th June – Commemoration Ball at Oriel College, Oxford, with Tony. [That night we were dancing an energetic Gay Gordons and my piece of false hair spun across the ballroom floor. Tony had to go grubbing around for it; put a bit of a damper on proceedings!]

I found myself an agent, Miss Bracewell, a faded blonde with buck teeth and horn-rimmed glasses. Got copies of the photos John Brown took, and hawked them round producers and directors, with my measurements and phone number on the back. She sent me to a few auditions, most of them for church-connected productions who didn't offer to pay more than a pittance. I played in Fry's *Boy With a Cart* and *Murder in the Cathedral* about Thomas a Becket. Better a small part than no part at all.

I met a Jewish boy, Henry Newman, tall, dark, thin, looked a bit like Frank Sinatra. He always wore a black pork-pie hat. He had the most marvellous sense of humour. He shared a basement flat in Maida Vale with Larry Hagman (who later became the legendary JR from Dallas). The walls were dead matt black, the only relief was jazzy mobiles hanging from the black ceilings! Larry was in the chorus of *South Pacific*, his mother, Mary Martin, played the lead and Enzio Pinza sang the part of the French planter. Just about the most exciting musical I've ever seen. The moving song 'Bali Hai', was a smash hit, in fact all the songs were.

To me Larry's pale blue eyes and fair curly hair were insipid beside Henry's magnetism. We used to go to the actor Theodore Bikel's place on a Sunday. He played the balalaika and sang old Russian folk songs. He was acting with Peter Ustinov in his play *The Love of Four Colonels*. Theresa Jewell was a good friend who I saw often after we left RADA. Many of the men we fancied were gay, but we naively had no idea. At one party we went to, it was getting late, and we'd been having a good old heart-to-heart talk up in a bedroom. We crept downstairs to phone for a taxi. Shock-horror, all these gorgeous men were sprawled around in various poses, copulating like mad … but with each other. We were so embarrassed!

I remember a strange evening with Theresa and her friend from Wales, Mary. The latter had an older man friend, who was a bit mysterious. We all came in late from a show, and he promised to cook us woodcock in wine, which sounded exotic. Neither of us could cook, of course. While we waited for the woodcock to marinate, he offered to hypnotise us. We were a bit dubious but, having had a few drinks, we were easy to persuade.

He hypnotised Mary first, since apparently she was a 'natural'. Soon he had her babbling like a two-year-old, then six years old, then nine years – it was most entertaining. Then he snapped her out of it and she refused to believe that she had regressed. Then he hypnotised me. I had no recollection afterwards, but apparently the same sort of thing happened. Theresa refused point blank, so we just settled down chatting and occasionally poking at the wizened little birds. I had what I can only describe as an hallucination: I'm in a house overlooking the sea, above high cliffs, waves crashing below the old wooden window, polished floors, rugs, there's a dark woman, she's angry.

'This is so weird!' I begin to describe what I'm seeing.

Mary's lover turns white. 'It's my hotel!' he blurts out. 'My … my…'

Mary looks at him. 'Your what?'

'My wife,' he stammers.

'You didn't tell me you were married!'

Then they went into the bedroom and argued. Theresa stared at me. 'What happened there?' To this day I can't explain it. The only possible answer is that somehow his hypnotising me caused a kind of psychic connection, and when he woke me up I was still on the wavelength, and his wife was trying to reach him. We never did eat those birds and they burnt to a crisp. I reckon I did Mary a favour. He was two-timing her, while she was besotted with him and already making plans to get married. She threw him out.

Soon after leaving RADA I started working for Leichner, the make up people. In those days most actors still used stick grease paints. Max Factor had started a new trend, pancake make up, and Leichner were experimenting with base in jars, as a cream. They wanted me to do facials – half the face, then instruct clients how to make up the other half. Sounds good in theory, but the results were often hilarious, if not ridiculous. A middle-aged lady would come in. I'd clean off her make up with remover (often leaving a tidemark of dirt at the neckline), give her a most beautiful look on one side, straightening a crooked nose, hiding bags under the eyes, lightening dark blotches, and leave her to it! The often short-sighted person, with slightly uncertain fingers, managed putting on the base and rouge on the other side, but eye shadow, liner and mascara, oh dear!

Mr Leichner, an Einstein clone with his wild hair, got the message and changed his tactics. Really all he wanted was to sell his new products, and all these elderly ladies were not the best adverts. So that was the end of my job. Before I left there, I bought a tin tool box, stencilled my name on it, and filled it with every kind of grease paint plus glue for false hair, false eyelashes, powder puffs, off-white face powder, cold cream, mirror, curlers, kirby grips for pinning up the hair, a stocking top cut off and tied for use as a cap under wigs (after a show you removed the grips and your head would be covered with little worm-casts like Topsy). It was the fashion for actors to use tool boxes for make up. Now I felt like a real pro!

My next job was scrubbing the floors at Queen Charlotte's Hospital. Unfortunately the old knee injury kicked in and I was forced to retire as a charlady. Work at a sandwich bar in Knightsbridge was next. The guardsmen used to come in sometimes. One of them was an amateur graphologist. I guessed this was something obscene, but he explained it was the study of handwriting. He wanted me to give him a sample of mine but I refused, in case it gave him some kind of hold over me. I worked in the Lyons ice cream factory a couple of nights. All of us had to be available for any auditions, so it was difficult to earn much money. My parents were agitating for a return on their investment, it was getting on my nerves.

There was an exhibition of artefacts from Tutenkhamun's tomb. His three sarcophagi, the innermost one gleaming with gold and turquoise, all the unbelievably fresh-looking pieces of jewellery and furniture made a great impression on us all. Eye make up became extreme, slanting black eye liner at the corners, blue or turquoise eye shadow. I went and had my long hair cut off in an attractive urchin cut, like Leslie Caron in *Gigi*.

Friday 10th July – Booked to start with Alan Hay, manager of the Theatre Royal Repertory Company in Huddersfield. It was in answer to an advert in *The Stage* for an ASM/Small Parts. At £7.10 per week! I'd sent off my most glamorous photo with long hair.

Monday 20th July – Off by train to Huddersfield. [They were cross with me when I arrived with short hair.] I'm cast as the maid in Emlyn Williams's *Night Must Fall*, with Leslie French as the porter/murderer, and Louise Hampton as the old lady who's murdered. He is very sinister. I have to learn the stage management bit in a hurry. Mend fuses, put plugs on things, work the sound effects, open and close the curtains! [Our course did not include stage management.]

Mon 27th July – Opening night. Leslie French very effective, especially when he sings 'Mighty Like a Rose' as he's about to do her in! I'm very nervous but am too busy to think about it.

Tuesday 28th July – Rehearse *Waters of the Moon*. I play Tonetta the Italian girl. [That's why they engaged me, because in my photo I had long hair and looked Italian.] I put on dark make up and lots of black eye liner.

Monday 3rd August – Opening night. It goes off well. I have a nice part, so much to do backstage, no time to be nervous. I have to walk home late at night through the sleazy back streets to my dingy flat. It smells funny.

Next day I ask one of the other actors about that area – he says it's the 'red-light' district of Huddersfield! No wonder men propositioned me on the way home. The following weekend Jeremy comes to stay with me. He looks aghast at the khaki-coloured décor but is too polite to say anything.

I find some other digs, Pond House, Mold Green, lovely fresh air, green fields. There really is a pond, right up above the smog, on the hillside. I love it there, especially the big, motherly landlady. A wonderful cook, her Yorkshire puddings are unequalled. Separate little pikelets served before the roast, crisp with large dollops of gravy. One of the other lodgers is a comedian-in-training; he asks me to listen to his jokes. I can't laugh, he isn't funny at all. Most embarrassing. I even try the actor's standby, agitating the muscles of the diaphragm to cause laughter, but it rings hollow. There's a market every Saturday, and with my first week's pay I buy a dress, the first from my own earnings, acid green cotton with horizontal black stripes.

Monday 10th August – Open in *The Housemaster* by Ian Hay. Jack Hulbert is the star. I play the maid. He's very nice, laid back, not snobbish like a lot of the so-called stars. [He was a very popular actor, known for his long chin. His sister was Cicely Courtneidge. They acted in comedies and revues, and featured in their own radio show.]

Monday 17th August – Open in *Whodunnit*, a frightful farce, with Claude Hulbert, a cousin of Jack, but he's dreadful!

Tuesday 18th August – Rehearse *Love from a Stranger* with Robert Beatty and Helen Shingler. She's a well-known TV star. He is a rugged Canadian actor, has made some good films.

Saturday 29th August – After the two shows, I'm busy putting away the props. They call me on stage, sing Happy Birthday, and give me a lovely pure silk scarf, emerald green graduating to pale brown. There's a cake as well, I'm so touched. It's my 21st, and I thought no one knew! Mummy must have phoned Alan Hay.

The diary then becomes a list of names and phone numbers. We went on tour with *Love from a Stranger*, Dudley, Peterborough, all Midland theatres. Then we did the same with *The Housemaster*. A succession of awful digs. In Peterborough I was playing darts in the pub after the show. One of the stage hands had been eyeing me. His dart ricocheted and hit me in the thigh. He apologised, we started chatting, he bought me a beer. I found myself locked out of my digs and so we eventually ended up on the shiny horsehair casting couch in Jack Hulbert's dressing room! Kept on falling off it too. There was usually a big social gulf between the actors and stage hands, but I was an ASM, neither one thing nor the other, and pretty lonely most of the time. We kept in touch by phone for a while, but there was no future in it.

We crossed the Irish sea by ferry, very rough going! Dublin was charming, spacious, grey stone classical-style buildings, lots of green parks. I'd been reading O'Casey, James Joyce, really filling myself with Irishness. Our digs were a different story. We had the misfortune to be the first-time lodgers of a couple of gays. They didn't know how to cook, served fish and chips, and the fish was barely defrosted. The sitting room was awash with broad red and white striped satin covers and curtains. They kept a monkey in an old fridge ... the door was propped open, but it didn't seem to be a suitable place to keep him. We moved out the next day.

Everyone said Irish tweed was the best, so I wandered down to the quayside one Saturday afternoon. There were open trestles with lengths arranged, I bought some red tweed, and further along there was beautiful handmade silver jewellery. I bought a pair of silver and jade earrings. A little crowd of beshawled, bare-footed crones had gathered round on hearing my dulcet English tones. They were muttering crossly in Erse and giving me dirty looks, a couple of stones were thrown at me from the back of the group. I retreated up the hill, they followed me jeering. I started running and reached the sanctuary of the castle. The local garda (police) escorted me back down the hill to the theatre, where the matinee performance was just beginning. I was just in time to change into my maid's uniform and dash on stage.

Another day the cast were taken on a trip to Bray, on jaunting carts (pony and trap), and were supposed to kiss the Blarney stone.

You had to twist yourself upside down to do it, so I contented myself with kissing the bit I could easily reach. Then we were taken round the Guinness brewery and given tiny little silver tankards, with samples of the brew – I thought it tasted horrible. When I asked what it was made of they said, 'Rats and Liffey water'! The river was pretty dirty, so no wonder it was awful.

Our stint ended and once more we had that rough ferry trip to Liverpool and carried on the tour round the Midlands, ending up at Golders Green Hippodrome. My contract was not renewed, and I went on doing odd jobs and going to auditions.

I travelled by train to Welwyn Garden City for a job demonstrating jam. There were two men in the carriage with me, in typical city garb, bowler hats and umbrellas. One had a nice face, but his skin was badly puckered, perhaps from plastic surgery. On the return train the same two men joined me. The older man left the train quite soon, but the younger one got out at Belsize Park, my stop (I was now living with my parents in Haverstock Hill). We looked at each other and smiled. He said, 'This looks like fate! Won't you have a cup of coffee with me?' So I did!

He was very well spoken and it seemed a harmless request. His name was Alex and he was a solicitor. We went out a few times. I discovered he had been a pilot and had had to bail out of his plane, which explained his skin. He bought me a pearl ring. We became engaged, and it was announced in the *Times*. One day we went to Burnham Beeches. It was autumn and there were huge piles of copper leaves. He kissed me. It wasn't a passionate kiss, more of a peck. I felt let down somehow...

That night I had a nightmare. He followed me and the leaves whispered eerily, then his hands were around my neck and squeezing hard. I woke up screaming, clutching my throat. My mother rushed in; I told her he was trying to kill me. She said maybe there was something about the relationship that I had ignored and my subconscious was trying to alert me to it. Later I went over the previous day, his maidenly kiss ... yes, that was it, he didn't want me physically, it appeared to be more of a duty. I imagined how a man with his disfigurement might really feel – perhaps he had been maimed emotionally, had another woman shown disgust? I envisioned the years to come, the frigid lifestyle, off to the City every day, all passion gone in stifling boredom. Would he really allow me to carry on acting after we were married?

Feeling very cruel, I broke off the engagement. I couldn't bring myself to tell him the real reason why, I just said I felt I was too young to think of marriage. More temporary jobs followed. I worked at Wilson's Bookshop in Hampstead, I loved that job! Used to go for drinks with friends after work at the Duke of Hamilton pub round the corner.

One day in Piccadilly I saw a madman pursued by warders in white overalls. He was bald, with staring eyes and a slobbering, loose mouth, wearing a shirt with a striped jersey, no trousers or underpants, white hairy legs and boots! They were carrying a straitjacket – it was straight out of a Mack Sennett Keystone Kops film, funny yet terrifying.

I went out with Hilary Evans, Dik's brother, for a while. I found him very attractive, but I felt guilty about deceiving Dik and let it peter out. I was still seeing Jeremy, but there was no spark, so I let him see me snogging some stranger at a party on board a barge one night and he dumped me. I didn't have the heart to tell him he bored me stiff!

On New Year's Eve my father and I were on our balcony watching fireworks. A lone piper started playing in the distance. All the finest laments. It was so unearthly and beautiful. The piper was homesick for Scotland, and so was my father. We both stood with tears in our eyes. Almost the only moment of communion we ever shared.

1954

On Thursday 11th February I started working at Murray Hutchins, solicitors, in Birchin Lane, Cheapside. I said I knew how to work a switchboard – well, I had played a switchboard operator in *Counsellor-at-Law* at RADA! It was a five-line lever board and it only took me half an hour to get the hang of it. Angela Foa worked there, an Anglo-Portuguese girl who was really sweet. She asked me to dinner and gave me tossed salad with home-made dressing, I was a non-cook at that stage, and the nonchalant way she managed the wooden salad servers impressed me no end. I couldn't stand the sardines, though.

I was still going to the Alliance Française occasionally and met Ian there. He was the most relaxed person I had ever met, which was most appealing after the exaggerated mannerisms of my actor friends. He was a veterinary student from Gloucester. We went out together a few times, and even got as far as discussing marriage. I spent a weekend with him at a hotel near his college. In those days you had to be married if you booked a double room, so I found a curtain ring at Woolworth's and bound cotton round it so it seemed to fit.

Once in our room, all the emotional stress of arranging a 'dirty weekend' (pretending to my parents I was going to stay with a girl friend), kicked in and I started the curse early. It was Sunday, no shops open, and I had no sanitary towels (sugar tommies as Nan called them, Signals slang). I don't know where he found them, but he did. It certainly put a damper on things. I would have thought that, being a vet, he would take such things in his stride.

We met again later that month at a hotel in London. He began to explain he loved me but he was on the horns of a dilemma. He had a mistress who was much older than him, whom he knew well and was 'comfortable with'. Then there was me. He said it was like comparing a soft feather bed to a springy new mattress! This amused me; I said I hoped I was the springy mattress. We parted amicably; you couldn't get upset with him he was such a lazy, likeable chap.

While working at the bookshop in Hampstead I had met Tony Payne and Gordon Price, friends of John O'Brian. They had worked together out in the Sudan as policemen, and had worked up a comedy routine which involved Gordon reciting 'The yellow eye of the little green god', by Rudyard Kipling. Tony came on and interrupted, 'I say, I say, I say!' 'Yes, what is it?' 'What is it that has eighty tits and sings?' 'I don't know, what is it etc...' 'Luton Girls Choir!' or 'What is it that has sixteen legs and flies?' 'Eight pairs of trousers!' The way they mimicked the old time music hall routine was side-splittingly funny. They had a strange little dance step, a kind of mince, which they kept going all the time.

At another party I was sitting on the floor next to a pretty American blonde. We watched a gay parody of Anna Pavlova's dance 'The Dying Swan'. This poor swan was trying to give birth to an enormous yellow egg. Eventually it plopped out to great applause. I started chatting to this girl, and it turned out she was Shelley Winters: in those days she was a famous film star (you might have seen her as the plump swimmer in the 'Poseidon Adventure', which won her an Oscar), married to Italian Vittorio Gassman, also a well-known film actor. So very pretty, lovely skin, curly short hair like a chrysanthemum, and quite unaffected by her fame. She was with John Gregson, a British screen heartthrob. I fancied him, dark eyes and hair, very macho.

Monday 22nd March – Audition for tour of *Me and My Gal*. Ring Dennis Vance, TV producer. Write letters to: Denis Carey, Bristol Old Vic, Frank Shelley, Oxford Playhouse, John Harrison, Nottingham Playhouse.

Soon after this my whole life changed. I had arranged to meet Dennis Vance at the Duke of Hamilton one lunchtime. I was gussied up, hair curly, blonde, nicely dressed, exquisite make-up. I sat nursing a beer for an hour or so. No Dennis – that bastard, if only he'd turned up I would have stayed in London, got on with my career. Peter Blandy came over to me and asked if I would like a drink. He said we'd met at one of Gordon Price's parties. I didn't remember him, but I was so furious at being stood up, I accepted.

He told me he was an ex RAF bomber pilot, just home from planting tea in India. He'd been to school at Wellington, then Oxford, was a Rugby and Cricket Blue. He was nice looking, warm hazel eyes, sensual mouth. He had no money at all, and was contemplating throwing himself off Westminster Bridge. I felt sorry for him! We went out a few times, started a wildly passionate affair. He was not very adventurous in bed, but was well equipped. I introduced him to the folks. They were not impressed. No money. No job. Mummy said he had a bad-tempered mouth, and he had a stammer (caused by being in a fire in Burma when he was five) ... but she liked the fact that he was well educated and came from a good County family. The more they demurred about our affair, the more I was determined to have him. Stubborn to the end!

I was still working at Murray Hutchins, fortunately, as my salary was the only money between us. I was disillusioned with the theatre world, the awful hanging around, waiting for auditions. We had been warned by our teachers, but each one of us believed it would be different for them. The parents nagged all the time: when was I going to earn some decent money (inferring I could pay them back for RADA and probably boarding school)? Peter got a job selling seed to farmers (on commission), and borrowed an old car from his friend, Tony Trevor-Roper. He applied for a job in Uganda.

We went down to Wales to meet his family. His mother was a Lloyd, her father started the breed of white Welsh mountain pony, and she used to go around all the agricultural shows judging pony events. They had a farm at Llandovery in Camarthenshire. Colonel Raleigh Blandy, late of the Gurkhas, was much older than his wife. He sat all day long eating toffee, and there were brown liver spots all over his tanned skin. She was nice but rather abrupt and bossy.

Near the farm was a vast mansion, Kyng Hordy, belonging to Lorna Blandy's elder brother. It had the usual ghosts, a wailing nun, and must have been impossible to keep up without a huge income and many servants. Lorna served up the best roast lamb I have ever tasted. I met Martin and Adrian, Peter's brother Richard's children, they were at school in the UK and he and his wife were in Malawi running a copper mine. There was a very old lady, Aunt Nest, who insisted on driving all over the place, but was 90 and half blind!

I discovered more about the way of life Peter had left behind at Ootecamund (Ooty) in southern India. When he came home from work he would sit down and his boots would be pulled off by one of his many servants. Often he would arrive home from the club at midnight and shout, 'Twelve sahibs for dinner.' An instant curry would have to be served! He had his own racehorse, 'Quaker Oats', and used to race him at gymkhanas. He played rugby, and cricket for prestigious planter teams. He was also having an affair with a blonde married woman.

At the All India Rugby Final Ball, his friend Paddy Grant was discovered having it off in the garden with the French Consul's wife ... unfortunately it was the French Consul who found them! A fight ensued, and Peter, as captain of the team, tried to mediate, but then he got involved in the fight and the result of the melée was a court case where they were charged with assault. He got the sack, but Paddy stayed on. He was very bitter about this.

He was very proud of the fact that Raleigh Blandy was descended from Sir Robert Peel, the prime minister who originated the Metropolitan Police, which is why they used to be called 'peelers'. Another branch of the family lived in Madeira and produced Blandy's Madeira (sherry).

I have a strange feeling that *I* actually proposed to Peter, sitting on high bar stools in the below-street-level Corkscrew Club. Several Pimm's must have inspired that, but I was tired of hanging around, what were we waiting for? It was obvious that no money was going to come our way in the near future.

The night before we married we went to the Duke of Wellington pub in Knightsbridge. We met a rich naval widow, who discovered we didn't even have a wedding ring (we were so impoverished). She said she had many rings, and insisted we use hers ... took us back to her flat. She had a sort of shrine to her late husband, flower-bedecked, and she opened her wardrobe. She had 64 pairs of shoes!

Saturday 12th June – Peter and I are married at Kensington Registry Office. I love him very much. I hope we make a success of our marriage. [I wore a cream and beige cotton dress, and a little cream half hat of artificial flowers. Our benefactress outshone everyone in deep sapphire velvet edged with swansdown, plus a matching hat and muff! She was a witness, and a very good friend. Barry Walters was the other one. No photographs, party or reception. Pretty sad kind of wedding.]

Sunday 13th June – Stay with Tony Trevor-Roper at his farm at Claydon Park. Then on to Guernsey to stay in Deenie Bale's cottage. [Deenie was a big, blowsy RAF widow with a generous heart.] There was a noisy brass double bed with a patchwork counterpane. A fisherman friend of hers supplied us with fish. I was handed a large blue lobster and told to cook it. I was horrified when Peter told me to plunge it into boiling water. I'm sure it screamed!

We went to the island of Herm for delicious strawberries and cream with scones for tea. Visited Sark, where the formidable Dame of Sark had held her own against the Nazis. Then it was back to reality in London. We stayed in Kensington, in a large basement flat, but we were existing on my meagre salary from Murray Hutchins. Peter started playing poker at clubs, and would sometimes crawl home at four in the morning, drunk, and throw handfuls of money onto the bed, as if that made up for everything.

One weekend we had invited a young friend to dinner. Peter was the expert curry maker, and he always made it very hot. Our fair-skinned blond guest wasn't used to curry, and when I saw him shaking a liberal amount of Tabasco sauce onto his plate I started to warn him, but Peter gave me a warning look not to say a word. Chris choked, coughed violently and couldn't breathe – Peter laughed his head off at the joke. Chris was allergic to the fiery stuff. We gave him water and thumped him on the back, and he eventually recovered, but from that moment the last vestige of respect for my husband disappeared. I was too proud to admit to my family that I'd made a disastrous mistake in marrying a coarse drunken libertine.

Saturday 25th December – Go to Pat and Clive's for Christmas lunch. Very good do, but ghastly mulled claret. A party in the evening at Richard and Sheila's. I drink too much and fall flat on my face [I wasn't used to much alcohol]. Sunday, lunch with Mummy and Daddy. Drinks with Adrian Ames. Party at Murray Milne's. Enjoyable. Am very careful to limit the hooch intake!

Monday 27th December – Lunch at the New Assam Curry Restaurant. Watch rugby match at Twickenham, Richmond v Harlequins, with Tony Psycopoulos (Cyclops) and Renee.

1955

Saturday 1st January – Peter gets his car [company car for the seed-selling job]. Last night at Richard the Pole's was a fiasco. We are served borscht (beetroot) soup and pig's knuckles with sauerkraut! Ugh! First time we see each other in evening dress. Drinks with les parents at the Duke of Hamilton. See the New Year in at Pat's (Hogmanay: First Footing). Go to the Blue Angel, very gay and giggly. Peter grazes the rear bumper of the car, at five in the morning ... the other car sped off.

27th April – Ante natal clinic. Bring specimen. Stamford Brook Station, Ealing Line [first mention of the pregnancy, now I couldn't very well leave him].

Saturday 14th May – Leave Murray Hutchins. God be praised! [By now I was sick almost constantly. The smell of sausages cooking was one of the worst causes. I was sick for seven and a half months. The doctors called it hyperemesis, but I think it was a fear of childbirth, a definite refusal of the mind to come to terms with pregnancy.]

Sunday 29th May – Pat's birthday. We set off for Entebbe. Peter has a job as assistant estate manager on a tea estate in Uganda. A terrible journey. An old DC3, the doors don't fit properly and the wind whistles past. We are squeezed in behind 36 motorbikes. We have engine trouble. Land in Malta. It's very hot. Our air hostess has shingles, she's tall and has to bend almost double as she creeps along past the honking bikes. More engine trouble, we are bouncing up and down and I'm very sick. Land in Luxor. Spend the night in a hotel with mosquito nets on the beds. I can't breathe with the heat. Take my mattress through to the outside stairwell. Am woken by a tall sentry in a fez and a nightie poking me with his gun. 'No sleep here! Memsahib!'
I can see the pyramids in the distance, but we have no time to

go there, only to inspect the badly cured camel-skin saddles and bags in the foyer. Sick as a dog. We fly to El Adhem in the western desert. The pilot is an old Wellingtonian, and lets Peter fly the plane. More engine trouble. Are given soggy fish and chips in the one-roomed hangar. Temperature 47 deg centigrade. Can hardly breathe. This was an emergency airstrip used by the RAF in the war.

Tuesday 31st May – Land in Entebbe. We stagger out and the man with us, who's in charge of the motorbikes, adjusts the bicycle clips around his ankles and organises the unloading. We are the employees of the Uganda Company, and take second place to the cargo. Drive out to Salama Tea Estate, 30 miles outside Kampala, the capital. Impression of women carrying loads on their heads, swaying along in bright Edwardian-style dresses with huge bustles, and everything so green, big plantains on either side of the road.

Sunday 12th June – Our first anniversary. Both very happy.

Sunday 26th June – Go to Mengo Hospital, have dysentery. We are staying in a horrible little cottage with an outside loo, a stinking cesspit full of pink jumping insects that hit you on the bottom as you sit there!

5th July – Am allowed to leave hospital. I can only keep food down when I'm there, away from the choo [loo]. I like the tiny little bananas grown in the Mission garden. Caroline Phillips, our manager's wife, is very kind, we are both studying Swahili. If I pass the exam I get 300 shillings (30 pounds), this will pay for my confinement. We are very hard up.

Sunday 10th July – Go to Kbanga Port on the banks of Lake Victoria. I take my sketching pad and watercolours. Try to capture the fuzzy mop heads of the papyrus plants that edge the water. I see two huge water snakes. They look like pythons. Lots of mosquitos. I'm taking Mepacrine anti-malarial pills, bright yellow with a vile bitter taste. There is a brewery here, makes 'Tusker', the beer with an elephant head on the label. We visit the White Rhino hotel.

Saturday 16th July – See Kobs play West Kenya (rugby). Peter played. Tea and drinks with the Gortons, an elderly couple who have a small coffee plantation nearby. Go to the Rugger Dance.

Monday 15th August – Go to hospital with a specimen.

Monday 29th August – My birthday. I make a soggy cake. Peter gives me a pair of shoes. [I go back to hospital with dysentery and sickness.]

Saturday 17th September – Leave hospital.

Friday 23rd September – Back in hospital.

Tuesday 27th September – See Dr Billington, now I have amoebic dysentery.

We move into a small, furnished company house, smelling of cockroaches and paraffin, with a smallish terraced garden on a hillside, backed by louring jungle. It's so hot. At least there is an inside bathroom and loo, and I can start to get better. Taking antibiotics. October 15th was Peter's birthday. We buy nappies and a woven Moses basket. The baby is due on November 10th.

Wednesday 23rd November – Caroline Jane Crerar Blandy born at 9.00 am. She yells lustily straight away. She's a most beautiful baby, smooth little face, thick wavy brown hair, rosy cheeks. Weight 5 lb 9¼ oz. I was worried she might have defects because of my constant illness, but somehow she's perfect, sweetest tiny nails! I had no advice about coping with labour, the Mission midwife said, 'Just keep your mouth open, so you don't tense up.' I felt terribly alone and afraid before she was born, no mother to comfort and advise.

The diary for the rest of 1955 is missing. In any case I think I was too busy with Jane, and later Fergus was on the way. A week after coming home from the hospital we weighed her on the potato scales at the local duka (shop). She was back to birth weight – I didn't have enough milk. Back to the hospital. They began supplementing my milk with formula, and she began to thrive.

For 1956 there are only fragments of my journal:

Monday 26th November – Rains all morning. Rest of the day blissfully cool. Take Jane for a walk in the push chair. [Jane started to walk at nine months, such an adventurous little thing.]

Tuesday 27th November – Had an unpleasant dream last night. Peter asked me for a divorce, said we should have waited longer before marrying. He wanted to marry my sister Pat instead. I warn her that, as she and I are so much alike, it would be a failure, P and I having so little in common. Woke up feeling uneasy and unwell. [I am now eight months pregnant with Fergus.] Spent the rest of the day in a state of mental and physical malaise. Probably caused by indigestion! Also the mention in Mummy's letter that Pat's divorce from Clive Montague Brooks would become absolute in six weeks time. Jane has the 'runs' and is consequently fretful. P goes shopping in Kampala. Am reading A.J. Cronin's autobiography, seems a nice person, lucky to find a re-belief in God, wish I could.

29th November – The Kabaka of Uganda (King Freddy) pays an unofficial visit to our estate. Meets all the bwanas (male bosses), of course, but not the wives. Rosie, my ayah, saw him when taking Jane out for a walk, most excited! Seven chicks hatch out.

Friday 30th November – Caroline Phillips, the manager's wife, and I go into Entebbe to take our Elementary Swahili Exam. We wait for ages. On comparing notes, we both seem to have had one really baffling sentence, while the rest went swimmingly. There were three examiners, a be-fezzed elderly one, probably from Mombasa or Dar-es-Salaam, a European, and one who looked Javanese. P goes off to watch the England v Scotland rugby match, and a stag dinner in the evening. I sign the Governor's Book, and notice lots of very impressive and pompous English dignitaries, then one entry: Mr Joe Kowanalika of Joe's Petrol Station. It looked so incongruous! The old hen has a broken leg. The garden boy kills it for dinner.

Sunday 2nd December – Jane isn't well, her temperature is 101, so we don't go to the McWilliams. P plays cricket all day at Lugazi. I finish reading *Mr Smith* by Louis Bromfield. Insightful, but written only from the male point of view.

Tuesday 4th December – Hannington the dispenser gives Jane a penicillin injection. He says she has tonsillitis, she's been better today and her temp. has gone down. Yesterday Dereck Emery and Bob Mackay turn up. They were going to stay with John Mortimer Jones (they've been thrown out of their house and have nowhere to stay). As we have two spare beds it seems more convenient for them to stay with us. They were loaded up with meat and radios.

    A bombshell: Rosie, the ayah has been told she has gonorrhea! Probably has had it since I employed her – horrors! Hannington says they all have it. When I engaged her I asked if she was clean inside (I didn't know how to phrase it delicately in Swahili) and she said she was. I sent her off to Mulago Hospital, pray God they cure her! There's an outbreak of rabies at Entebbe. Dereck and Bob have brought their cook, William. An enormous fellow, who has just been cured of 'wheelbarrow elephantiasis' (swollen balls) ... what next?

Friday 7th December – Rosie returns. She said she didn't know she had G.

Saturday 8th December – Rosie is vindicated! Hannington sends a note to say it isn't the dreaded G., but only bad menstrual trouble. So she's reinstated, and I give her a photo of her and Jane to cement things. In the evening Hugh and Caroline, and John Mortimer Jones, come to dinner. I had given Cherubino [the houseboy] a half day off, so gawky William had to serve. P is furious, and the leg of lamb doesn't stretch very far, no ice-cold water for their whisky, no nuts to eat, I'm in disgrace! Nevertheless we had a pleasant evening. At least the trifle was nice.

Sunday 9th December – The unpleasant Watsons don't turn up because of a terrific storm blowing. I'm glad. His 'Gay Lothario' manner, flickering eyebrows and trap-like mouth are annoying. I'd baked ham with honey glaze and all (although the glaze had run down the sides and was seen no more). Yesterday I had bearing down pains, probably due to the fact that I've had to wash nappies all week – Rosie being away, and male servants refuse to wash female babies nappies, just as they won't wash female adult panties. So glad Rosie came back today, she really is a treasure, I wouldn't let her go, even if she had G! Dereck and Bob went to the Police Ball yesterday and returned this evening.

Six baby chickens were eaten and mauled and left to die by some animal on Friday night. The askari [night watchman] didn't seem to have noticed anything (he wouldn't!). The little carcases had teeth marks on them –might be a civet cat, feral cat, jackal ... we are so near the jungle rearing over us. Tonight in bed I hear an awful yowling in the small hours and leap out of bed, to let Butch out, but P says no, it might be a panther.

Friday 14th December – We set a trap for the chicken stealer. Some were put in wire netting on boxes raised from the ground. The marauder pulled some through on Wednesday night. The askari called us and we found a huge feral cat glaring in the torchlight. P shot him. Jane is getting more teeth. Letter from Mummy enclosing a fiver. The zinnias planted are coming up, they look quite weedy, unlike the wonderful photo on the packet. Last night the askari accused Cherubino of stealing two debbies [empty paraffin tins]. The usual noisy altercation – no one can prove anything.

Saturday 16th December – Calling the kitchen toto at teatime my voice died away, and an awful stillness remained. Away upon the left, on the brow of the thick jungle behind the house, a large monkey suddenly leapt down from a great height to the bushy undergrowth. A tiny breeze whispered on my cheek. I stood in the shade of our one respectably large tree. Beyond it everything shimmered dryly. A feeling of dread.

In the evening, fireflies darted by the water tank. I sat on the steps for a few minutes, unwilling to go back to the stuffy, brightly lit sitting room. I've been reading too much, my eyes are dry and strained. Red flowers beside the door, I don't know their name, vivid against the blue darkness, they have the artificiality of colours under city lights, neon lights. I'm sick of myself, of the hot weighty thing that is my burden. Tired of inaction, mental and physical.

Later a note arrived from Caroline, we have both passed the Swahili exam. Xmas is getting near, so much to remember. We ran out of potatoes and butter again this week. P says if he did his job the way I do mine, he would get the sack. I agree. My brain is like mush.

25th December – Xmas Day. Difference of opinion as to when to start cooking the duck and goose. I say 12 o'clock, P says one. I follow his directive. We eat at 3.45. Birds not quite cooked. The beastly wood-burning oven plays up again, it's blocked up with tar and smoking. Still, it was a pretty good meal. We poured Drambuie over the pudding and there was a magnificent flame! Dereck Emery, Lloyd Thomas, Malcolm Davis, Bob Mackay and his fiancée Jean (the latter came late, I thought they'd never arrive). P served his well-known potent Pimm's. Noisy great fun. Jane trotted around while we were in the dining room and ate potato chips, cheese biscuits, currants and nuts and cigarette ends! Dereck gave us a music box which played 'Lili', she threw it on the floor hoping to produce music by this method. They also gave her a polar bear. Butch also snaffled the various eats that Jane left.

Lloyd and I had a fierce argument about the stage. He thought it a poor show that no actors of renown bother to come to Kenya to start a professional theatre. I mentioned the Donovan Maule Theatre in Nairobi, he said they used mainly amateur actors. I begged to differ. I know they use professionals who've settled in the country: Tim Bungay and Mike Mcabe, for instance? [There was no pro theatre in Uganda, so we would always have to go to Nairobi for 'culture'.]

26th December – Boxing Day. We go into Kampala. Lunch at the City Bar, then on to the Police Club for black velvets (Guinness and champagne). Peter Wilkins is in great form –he was burgled on Xmas Eve and hasn't got a thing left, just the shirt and shorts he was wearing. Luckily he's insured. Now he's throwing care to the winds! The Fairbrothers arrive, Pauline looks fresh and attractive. We have the usual irritating discussion, comparing our respective babies' advances in size and aptitude. Ted Seed is pretty high, draping his tall thin form around anything feminine. Later we go on to Lubowa, say hullo to the Tylers. They were married for ten years and had no children so they adopt one and bingo she's pregnant! The men play tennis drunkenly. A session of lier-dice. Party at Kololo flat. Full of Caltex people. The police crowd arrive, and the party livens up. Peter Wilkins now wears only a singlet and shorts. Robin Fairrie comes with his dogs.

Friday 28th December – We go to the Blind School for prize giving. They play football with a small rubber ball which has a bell inside it. They are very agile. Francis Griffiths runs the Blind School. He and his wife and two children live in the cottage we vacated – poor souls! Baganda women drift onto the field. What colours, a candy pink Edwardian-style frock with a wide orange sash, cerise with scarlet, they should clash, but they don't! Fat Kagwa the supervisor wants to join in the tug-of-war, but his qualifications are too overwhelming … Jane behaves well, chews grass.

Saturday 29th December – P goes into Kampala for the Rugger Dance – I don't.

Sunday 30th December – Ted Seed and Alison come over for curry lunch. He goes off to Nairobi, then on to Gulu to learn Acholi. Everyone is somnolent.

Monday 31st December – Shopping. All the things for the new baby are ready (I hope!) New Year's Ball at the Top Club. Fancy dress and barbecue. I drink beer, champagne, gin … Lots of very good costumes – Arab League, Piccadilly Circus, Shanks Royal Flush, Nudist Camp, Pyjama Game. I rock and roll with Dereck Emery.

1957

Monday 7th January – Go into Kampala with Caroline Phillips and Jane. They have polio shots. I don't as I've already had it. Jane is brave, hardly squeaks! Letter from Mummy. They've moved to an unfurnished flat, No. 32A Frognal. Pat's children are to be sent to the Actors' Orphanage – what a terrible shame, they are delightful children. Clive, I hear, is marrying again, an actress he met on tour. How can an out-of-work actor pay maintenance and keep a new wife? Pat says she leads a gay life ... Ay di mi!

Thursday 10th January – The Carr family were expected for lunch, but only he comes. We needn't have killed the cock. The garden boy killed the wrong one, it should have been a hen! P is furious with me. Jane now waves goodbye and points at objects as we name them. Have been reading Daphne Fielding's book *Mercury Presides.* I feel just like her, at the end of her pregnancy she rips up all her maternity clothes! I've been hauling out my pre-pregnancy tatty clothes and trying to alter them, or at least sew on buttons, to have a new dress! Have been having erotic dreams, I suppose because the baby presses as though he/she wants to come out.

Tuesday 15th January – Just got up after two days in bed with a bad cold. Felt like someone out of Dante's Inferno, perspiring, so hot from the heat and a temperature! Oh! To be in chilly England! I'd even welcome chilblains ... Jane is making phlegmy noises, hope she doesn't get it too. I do take precautions and go around like a bandit with a hanky draped over my nose. On Friday I went for a blood test. I'm rhesus negative so they have to start testing for antibodies. Read an article in a mag. which says they may have to drain all the blood out of the baby's body and replace it with positive blood.

Have sown flower seeds indiscriminately all over our so-called garden. One can't do much with this rocky plateau. Stocks, delphiniums, and some unpronounceable ones, The zinnias were most disappointing. 'Put not your Faith in Seed Packet pictures!' Have bored holes in two ex-paint cans and planted maidenhair ferns taken from the jungle at the back of our house. One is magnificent. P says Monsieur L'Oiseau is coming to dinner on Friday at the Phillips' house. They are away so we will have to entertain him. My French is very rusty. P takes Jane into Kampala for her first diphtheria injection. Cherubino isn't at the planned rendezvous so he has to come home without him.

Friday 18th January – What a disaster! M. L'Oiseau is charming but speaks no English. My French deserts me. Every word comes out as Swahili, have been swotting it so hard. P is disgusted with me. Another failure to chalk up on the blackboard of my inadequacy. He has to attempt conversation with his schoolboy version. At least the food is all right because the Phillips' cook is an expert.

Saturday 19th January – Still no Cherubino. The kitchen toto is coping manfully, but it's far too much for him.

Saturday 26th January – Cherubino comes back, thank God!

Monday 28th January – Have to go into hospital, am violently sick. I thought I'd started off labour pains, but anyway Dr Chance says I should stay in hospital in case ... I asked him to induce labour but he says it's too risky. Letter from Pat, wonderful to hear from her instead of about her – is now completely free of Clive. Children are definitely going into the Actors' Orphanage. Jane's molar is nearly through.

Saturday 2nd February – Guinea fowl eggs are hatching out. Jane has the runs. We bought her some red sandals, she took to them at once, struts around very proud! Spent some time looking for a pair for myself, P champing at the bit. While we were at the butcher's I slipped into Nadia's and found a pair. One never has time to amble round the (few) shops.

Quite a lot of rain the last few days – bliss! On Thursday all the estate managers ploughed, waltzed, and slewed through the lousy potholed roads to the Rivers' house for dinner. Poor Ray Rivers arrived at 9.30 as we were all leaving! He'd been bogged down in the mud. Last night we went to see *Private's Progress*, rather naughty! Ian Carmichael not as good as usual. In the car with the others we discussed marriage proposals. P and I had to admit we couldn't remember who proposed to whom.

Thursday 7th February – P brought me into Kampala to stay with the Laws until things happen. Baby due yesterday. Went for another blood test, in the earlobe, rather painful! I've bought myself a white blouse, rather extravagant, but comforting to picture wearing it when I'm back to a normal size. In the evening John took Peggy and I to Fort Bell. Lots of launches there, including the Kabaka's. He drove up in his Daimler and nattered to John for a while. The lake was mirror still. Islands in the heat haze were every shade of grey, Japanesy … terrible smell from the brewery. They've had hippos galumphing in the reeds there lately. Sat on a spar of timber and listened to the marsh croaks, shrieks, burbles, splashes … love the papyrus mop heads!

Been reading *Anglo-Saxon Attitudes* by Angus Wilson. He certainly knows the semi-homo underworld which fringed on RADA. Also read *A World of Love* by Elizabeth Bowen. Letter from Mummy. TV seems to make a great difference to the parents' home life, helps to prevent the bored vacuum they have always endured with each other. Pat is back in favour, Nan is not, 'typical hard Army wife' M says.

Saturday 9th February – Six am this morning the pains started. Arrived at hospital at 7 am. Baby delivered at 12.30 pm. Weight 6 lb 9 oz. A boy – Hurray! I had no stitches. Ether was given towards the end, terrific help!

Tuesday 12th February – Fergus is doing well, as far as I can see. Milk coming in well, Lovely flowers from P, and also from the Gordons [Col. Gordon was our boss at the Uganda Co]. Today I feel almost normal, and ready to go home. Fergus has a funny little face, sometimes he looks like Danny Kaye, fair hair, eyebrows and lashes, light eyes sure to turn blue, aquiline nose [it will be], long fingers and toes. P brought Dereck and Malcolm to visit us on Sunday evening. They were most amusing! P had been left in his car in the factory compound by a drunken Mortimer Jones on Sunday morning. P 'came to' at 12 pm. Don't know what the old askaris must have thought? Why becoming a father has to result in such orgies ... One would imagine the man had done some of the hard labour himself! Caroline Phillips came to see me as well, brought Jane with her. She's well.

Friday 15th February – Peggy Law came to see me, gave me a lace hanky and some perfume. Have been reading *The Cornerstone* by Zoe Oldenbourg, and *Vile Bodies* by Evelyn Waugh. Also *Passage to India* by E.M. Forster. All absolutely brilliant! Chatted to a garrulous Scots woman from Nairobi, in the same ward. A long time since I spoke to one of this variety. The anxious to please air, fixed eye and bridling head ... She has bronchitis and is anxious to discuss it. There is a tree in one corner of the garden below my window, where the shamba [garden] boys, old men and women come to sit. They brew up matoke [green plantains], and cook posho [mealie meal], and hang their washing in the branches. Cut out pictures from English magazines are nailed to the trunk. There's also a little red clay figure of a man. Must have some tribal significance, a god, a devil, or some luckless headman doomed to a painful demise? Mengo Mission Hospital is in the oldest part of Kampala – perhaps the garden was part of a witchcraft cult ... now surrounded by the Christian Mission.

Sunday 17th February – Fergus is to be circumcised, poor little devil! P insists, says it's hygienic to have it done in Africa. I thought it was a Jewish fetish ... Last night I had a jaunt out. Jaunt is the right word. In the wretched one-seated estate van. I sat on the floor on a rubber cushion, am seriously worried as to whether my womb is upside down now. We go to a new restaurant, 'The Flamingo'. Gaudy red and white paper decorations, great sport for future flies, as they will not be taken down, but hang there forever ... They serve chicken curry à la Patel (chopped up into large pieces with an axe). Also chappatis, fish and chips and pudding or jelly! They don't have a liquor licence yet, so Malcolm does his comic waiter act: solemnly pours Dereck a soupçon from a water bottle shrouded in a napkin, Dereck holds the glass to his ear, sniffs the bouquet, sips the water with a true connoisseur's air, then nods slowly to Malcolm, who then reverently pours water into all our glasses. Mrs McPherson is there waiting for her husband, but I have to be back in the hospital in time to feed Fergus, and we callously drive past him, his car having broken down.

After the feed we go out again, to the Silver Springs Hotel. There are two very thin black cats. Wild-looking, belly close to the floor, they slither over the polished floors, thin shoulders hunched high over snaky body, flattened brutal heads. They seem to be stalking some invisible enemy, making sudden rushes from table to table.

Back at the hospital a party of tanned Germans arrive. They are very handsome and the nurses flutter around them. They were on safari, in a bus. Covered with cuts and bruises, broken ankles, malaria...

Monday 18th February – Letter from M, she has become a Presbyterian. I suppose it's better than being an agnostic? Dr Chance refused to circumcise Fergus. Said it was not necessary. I don't know what to do, P will be furious! I have tea with the Gordons, big honour.

Tuesday 19th February – Go home. Fergus weighs 6 lb 10¾ oz. Jane comes over from the Phillips. She hasn't forgotten me, and smiles radiantly! Giggles shyly. They say she was a model child, and have become very attached to her. We give them a travelling clock, and a purse to their child, Alison.

Thursday 21st February – See Kampala Amateurs in *The Deep Blue Sea*. Quite a good effort.

Saturday 23rd February – Bob and Jean come to lunch. They are engaged! I didn't notice the ring until Dorothy Gorton spotted it. Trust her! It will be a secret wedding (i.e. cheap) like ours.

Monday 25th February – Tennis at the Phillips, Margot Gordon is there. Fergus is being very good.

Tuesday 26th February – He weighs 7 lb 6½ oz. I seem to have plenty of milk so far. 12 oz in a week. Cor! Am very thirsty all the time. Have started to smoke. Letter from Gordon Price. What a disastrous life he has – cataclysms at every turn! Berry runs away from him, he loses his job, says Tony Payne is involved with a divorcee … surprise surprise!

Tuesday 5th March – Big drama – we catch a python in the hen run. 12 foot long, and thick! The askari spots him, and calls us. It's dark, so we take the torch, a gun, a whip, Grey Betteson comes too. P shoots it in the head, then they haul it out and drag it up into the garden. He ties the whip round its supposed neck, and tethers it under the verandah door. In the small hours Fergus wakes for a feed. I sit there and I can hear the python struggling to breathe, a horrible snoring sound. P thought it was dead. Next morning it appears to be, P wants to take a photo so we drape it over the little pick-up truck. Grey holds its head, I hold the middle on a forked branch, and the kitchen toto hangs onto the tail, at the back of the bacci. Next thing, it gives a gigantic wriggle, and pees all over the poor toto! P decides he's going to have shoes and a handbag made out of its admittedly handsome skin. Takes it down to the headman and asks him to tan it. [Months later they produced the handbag and shoes – they stank! We had to throw them away.]

Tuesday 2nd April – This week was in hospital with milk fever, malaria and pharyngitis. Fergus weighs 10½ lb. We've bought a Volkswagen. It's a marvellous improvement on the car I knew in Germany. Wonderful suspension, very important for these awful potholed murrum roads. Jane's recovering from a bad cold, her canine teeth are coming through. I've cut my hair short, back to the style I had at 18.

Saturday 6th April – P has gone off to Tororo to play rugger. Am reading *Mark Lambert's Supper* by Michael Innes. Good. We saw *Daddylonglegs* last night. Leslie Caron is fatter, almost tarty. Marvellous sets, what colours! Fergus sucks his thumb a lot, and scratches his poor nose. Jane's mutters begin to sound like words: 'Hullo', 'Deah', (there), 'Boy', it'll be fun when she's old enough to be read to, shall hunt up my treasured favourites for her. Fergus slept from 8 pm to 6 am this morning – great, let's see if he can keep it up tonight (he does). Jane did that at 3 months.

Sunday 7th April – Am neglecting the chickens horribly. Loathe going out into the glare of the afternoon, one is roasted. A recurrence of frustration about my ill-planned, ill-run life. It would be something if I could keep this diary up for a while – full of my vapid fancies and boring activities as it is ... have no one to talk to, no friend that I can trust. This *is* a good life, it's real, worthwhile. Give and take of affection. I can make or break our marriage. It's up to me to succeed at *this* career. Was my previous way of life so worthless? That wonderful, exhilarating independence, sense of buoyancy, I sucked it in without regard to quality – just smiling faces, an audience.

Friday 12th April – Cherubino was booted out on Monday. He had gone off on Saturday, and only returned Monday. His replacement is a gormless creature, but better than nothing. The toto is rather good. Bad shauri [trouble] with my so-called 'treasure', Rosie. Yesterday evening she was late, and we were due in Kampala to dine with the Phillips. What a nasty story it's uncovered. Not only is she no longer living with her husband, Katera, but she is now a prostitute, living with her pimp in Luga Labour lines! My indispensible, lovable ayah! I was very fond of her and she loved Jane – what led her to it? The sight of pretty trinkets in a European house? I never fined her for petty peccadillos, although the other wives fine their staff severely. P says the askaris will hound her off the estate.

Saturday 13th April – Fergus weighed 11 lb on Tuesday. That evening we left him with Peggy Law and we wined and dined with the Boshoffs. Smoked salmon and Chateauneuf du Pape. Mireille has a mind like mine – odd to think she is a Continental. She loved Newcastle. We have both agreed that intellectually inclined women can marry essentially 'physical' type men. It works. Wistful longings for poetry can be sublimated as long as the body is satisfied. [I meant sexually, but who was I kidding? Those days I was perpetually starved of sex and affection.] Turning to discussion of Art, we agreed that people who denigrate Picasso were mad, his amazing gifts, his discovery and use of African masks, of Cubism, influenced current design – clothes, furniture, carpets, walls, curtains, even architecture. Mireille has walked through his pottery factory in France.

Good news from the parents – Daddy has landed a job with Reichdrills, an American firm. £15,000 per year. Pat is writing a play for TV. Both Nan and Pat are at loggerheads with M. Letter from Freda Evans congratulating me on the new baby. [She was now Jane's godmother.] I feel a little twinge, how I would love to be there at Ridley, basking in the Evans charm! [Jane was christened at 9 months, Paddy Grant was the other godparent, stayed with us for a while.] Caroline Phillips goes home on Sunday. I shall miss her.

Sunday 14th April – See Caroline off at Entebbe Airport. Also Mike Hammerton [he was an attractive rugby-playing friend of P's who kissed me after a dance, an innocent peck, for which I was never, ever forgiven]. Both Jane and Fergus come with us. Jane trots around with her usual savoir faire, while Fergus displays stoic calm, even when the propellers rev up in an ear-splitting cacophany!

Friday 19th April – Nan is having another baby. Letter from Cecilia Collie in Kitale. She is delighted to be asked to be Fergus's godmother, but doesn't think she is a suitable person. Her own sons aren't christened yet, and she never goes to church … nowadays few people take their duties that seriously. I was under the impression that I was Catherine's godmother, and felt guilty because I hadn't done anything about it. I sent her a b'day present, and Nan wrote back acidly that I was not her godmother, so not to worry about it. Rugger at Nakivubu Stadium, very good game. We win. No injuries, except for Tinker Bell, the referee! Jane and Fergus both very good, both sleep in separate cars. Dinner at the City Bar.

We have four guests. Two of them sleep in the Phillips' guest house. Go to the Silver Springs Hotel. I'm in a hurry, as usual, fall, bruises, sprained toe, grazed elbow and knees, deep cut on the hip.

Saturday 20th April – Not able to go to the dance at the Top Club owing to my fall. Was hoping to see Barry McCurdy again there.

111

We had really danced together at the Springs. They played 'Singing in the Rain' and we spun around like Gene Kelly and Cyd Charisse! It was such fun!

Thursday 25th April – Fergus 11 lb 8 oz. He hasn't gained much. Jane was sick last night, and again in the car on the way to Kampala. Either teething or something she ate? Tea at the Bottles' [Harbottles]. Mrs H. makes a great fuss over her non-jelling jam.

Sunday 28th April – Shamba boy reports the loss of a hen, the foster mother of five chicks, he's sure the mate of our python has taken it. Perhaps we'll catch it on Monday? My cut is healing slowly. Col. Gordon is visiting the estate today.

Friday 3rd May – We find a puff adder curled up in the bottom of a beer crate of empty bottles! Jane had just been playing with the bottles – something made P pull out the bottles and he found it. Thank God she wasn't bitten. Juma the shamba boy killed it with a sharpened stake, just like a vampire! Fergus's Moses basket is put out under the tree every day. I've noticed strange red bite marks on him, in spite of the net draped over the basket. I examine the bedding and discover weird bugs, never seen anything like them before. To my horror I discover they are bedbugs! Where could they have come from? The poor little soul had been suffering and we had no idea. At night his basket is placed on the bed in the guest room. It has leather thongs placed crosswise instead of steel springs [riempies]. We take the bed out into the light. (The room is always dark because a verandah was built onto the house.) We find more bugs. Soak the whole lot in paraffin. All our beds have half tins of paraffin under the legs because of siafu [ants]. Now we put his basket in Jane's room.

Saturday 11th May – Jane, Fergus, new ayah, and I are all at the rugger match. Later we watch a boxing display, Uganda v Kenya. The Ugandans seem taller and fitter. Les Peach, the police heavyweight contender, knocks his opponent out in the second round. Another police man was Idi Amin, of ill fame, then a strapping young boxer, who easily beat his opponent. We go on to the Taboris Bar, which is great fun, except that John Law puts on his usual embarrassing drunken display, tipping water over Jean Mackay's dress. George, the Greek manager, says he won't allow him in there again.

16th May –Have written to Gordon Price, Barry Walters, Freda Evans, and Cecilia Collie. Have asked her to arrange for Fergus to be christened when we go to Kitale for the Rugger on May.

26th May – Jane climbs up on the dining room chairs now, so we have to put them against the wall, she's into everything. It's a problem trying to train her to sit on the potty, at the moment she is so sore from nappies and teething that I'm leaving her with a bare behind. Fergus has colic. Can't make up my mind whether to write down my inner feelings – I don't like the idea that I have nowhere to lock away this journal. Perhaps I can get rid of my foolish fears by writing them down and, in doing so, see how pointless they are.

Fergus, Malindi

At Meru tea estate

Rosie and Jane

The 12ft python, Salama

Michael, Meru

The rondavel at Meru

Our first tent at Meru, with temporary roof

The house at Meru being built

Saturday 18th May – P plays Rugger at Jinja. Says it's an awful game. Two people turn up late, and the referee is useless, he's depressed.

Sunday 19th May – Drive to Entebbe. Cold and rainy. Jane wants to go in the water, but it's quite rough. She goes round all the picnickers, exacting tribute in the form of biscuits and admiration. She really is extraordinarily self-possessed! Fergus is very good, bless him! P, still grumpy and hung-over, sat in the car all afternoon. I swam, or rather surfed! Later we had tea at the Victoria Hotel. Jane, now in dungarees, trotted off to the bar. There she scared a little girl much bigger than herself by bumping her with her tummy! When we got back, Michael the houseboy was drunk with native beer. P hit him.

Friday 24th May – Michael left yesterday. Another boy turns up, Alberto by name. Now the cook leaves, in sympathy with Michael, about time too. Jane, two shamba boys, the toto, and Alberto go off to the Bettesons' house through the narrow jungle defile. A weird procession! I bring up the rear. Jane is installed and seems quite happy, so I tiptoe off in case she thinks I'm deserting her.

Saturday 25th May – We set off for Kitale at 9 am. I breast feed Fergus in motion after we leave Jinja, and it isn't bad at all. At least it's all right if the road is smooth! Fortunately the roads to Kitale are good, and there's no rain. [All the roads were murrum in those days.] Stop for sandwiches at the Tororo Hotel, a lousy place, absolutely shenzi [awful].

Arrive at the Collies' at 2.30 pm. Very good going. No one to meet us, except the governess, Miss Thompson, as they expected us later. Finally Cecilia lopes over the lawn to us, babbling of gharries [cars] and manure. Harris, who's named after their Massey-Harris tractor, a sturdy little blond, quite a toughie, will also be christened tomorrow. We go to a dance at the Kitale Club. All the other men are wearing DJs, P and Duncan Collie in suits. Cecilia enjoys herself gossiping with odd bods, one nicknamed 'Bloody Mary', and a Mrs Bell who's been widowed three times and is married to her fourth! (Wonder how long he will last?) Large mouth, long black hair, screwed up on top, arty-looking. Then there's the Stumps. Mrs S is very swarthy, so the Collies call her 'the Black Stump' after Nevil Shute's Beyond the Black Stump. Am dragged into the Paul Jones, and various men tread on my toes! Of course P only deigns to dance with me once – how I hate going to dances and not dancing … we stick in the mud on the way back, and see an aardvark in the headlights.

Sunday 26th May – The proxy godfathers only turn up after the christening is over! Fergus and Harris are extremely good. Harris is hauled up and suspended over the font – his savoir faire is amazing! At the end the vicar says, 'You are one of the Family now,' and he says, 'Yes,' in a tone of voice that means 'of course I am'. Cecilia gives Fergus a prayer book. Very exciting rugby game at 3 pm. We just win, 19 – 18. Roads wet and very skiddy on the way back to Uganda. We overtake many of our team. Eat at the Ripon Falls Hotel at 10 pm. Arrive home at 12.30 pm. The toto tells us in a trembling voice that there's been a fire. The paraffin fridge caught fire, the sheet of hardboard behind it, all the boy's kanzus [long robes] and waistcoats, paintwork ruined, all the food inside the fridge boiled, ceilings of scullery, bathroom, and guest room blackened. Thank goodness Butch wasn't locked in or he would have suffocated!

Monday 27th May – More disaster! The Griffiths who live in the guest cottage told me they were sick of living out of tins, and would I sell them a hen? The temporary shamba boy brought a fowl to me to get the OK, and I was in a hurry getting ready for our trip, gave it a cursory glance, said kill it. It was our pedigree cock, not to be killed on any account! I only charged her 5 shillings instead of 10! P and I had a duel of words – he, the relentless accuser, piling up all my misdeeds. I am so conscious of them myself, there's no need to belabour the point. If we get an efficient servant the house takes on a gloss, but as soon as a sloppy one comes along, I don't really notice until it's too late and everything goes to pot! Later that night, overcome with misery, I weep over Fergus. At that moment P returns with Grey Betteson. He says, 'We'll talk later.' Of course, we don't talk later, we never do – at least Jane is glad to see me. P and Grey have been to the Gorton's Tea Estate. Two Indian family members have died of heart attacks, and great feasting is going on to placate the ancestors. The two of them are gorged on curry. I lie in bed and think of separation, divorce. I am so frustrated, all he wants is a good cook and bottle washer. The only time he ever makes love to me is when he's drunk, and then he's a lousy lover.

Surely a normal man would show some tenderness, warmth sometimes, not sleep like a log every night? I'm sure my housewifely abilities would improve because I'd be relaxed, happy. His excuse is that rugger exhausts him, he's just too sleepy, or he just says goodnight and turns away. Once I tried to slip into bed with him but he turned on me as if I was a whore – I'm his wife for God's sake! Single beds are a curse! He drinks too much beer, maybe he just can't do it? All he needs to do is just occasionally give me a hug, or a smile, or a word of appreciation.

Tuesday 28th May – Go shopping. Fergus has a smallpox vaccination.

Friday 30th May – Drinks with the Griffiths. Most amusing couple. We hear all about the 'Box'. You put three spots of your blood on a piece of blotting paper and send it off to people in Nairobi, and they claim to be able to diagnose your malady. If it's a surgical problem they tell you, or they cure whatever is wrong … I would love to try it, but I'm too healthy!

Saturday 1st June – Rugby match at Jinja. See Jinny Pook, she's pregnant again (the third). Dine at the Ripon Falls Hotel. Raw chicken – terrible service! Afterwards we plough back home in the rain. The Lanes are with us, she is sweet, and he is great fun.

Sunday 2nd June – They and the Griffiths are supposed to come to lunch with us. No one arrives. In the evening the MacPherson's drop in. P sees that the level in the whisky bottle has dropped – he thinks it must be the kitchen toto who's taking it.

Monday 3rd June – P takes the kitchen toto to the Gombololo Chief. He's beaten with a rhino-hide whip [sjambok]. I loathe the excessive violence, the piga-ings [beatings] that go on. We couldn't prove he'd taken the whisky … Jane isn't well, teeth as usual? Temp of 100 this morning, won't eat or drink, but better this afternoon. Hannington comes over to borrow the thermometer, says all the ones at the clinic are broken, has tried the Phillips, but Hugh is out (and Caroline away). Jane isn't well, and might get worse, and yet, for the lack of one, someone might fail to be treated in time. He looks at Jane and says he doesn't think she'll get worse, so then I let him take it. When

P comes back he's furious, 'Putting the bloody thieving watu [men] before my own child!' I'm sure Caroline would have done the same. Any way we've run out of butter so he storms out and says he'll have tea with someone else.

Tuesday 4th June – Fergus has a spotty rash. Hannington has returned the thermometer to us. Jane now has a temp. of 104, I'm so nervous I drop and break it!

Wednesday 5th June –Wake up wondering if she's still alive. I creep into her bedroom, full of dread, then I hear her tummy gurgling and I know she's still alive.

Thursday 6th June – Go into Kampala, see Dr Gordon Brown. He says it's teething, but she's better anyway! Fergus's rash is the vaccination, not measles as I feared.

Friday 7th June – Nicky, the Griffiths' youngest son, has fallen down the choo [loo]! The seat was dislodged somehow. Fortunately the drop was only 7 foot instead of the usual 20 foot. His grandmother lay down into the stinking pit, we held onto her ankles and she just managed to reach his fingers. Poor little soul! When we lived there the siafu [safari ants] got into the pit, and all the ghastly pink jumping things that lived in there started to try to get out while I was on the seat ... He seems none the worse for his ordeal, children are amazing! Their poodle bites our toto – what next?

   Later, in bed, I pluck up enough courage to speak to P. He says, 'The way to a man's heart is through his stomach.' So it's my culinary failings that turn him off, oh well, back to Mrs Beeton! Even though we have a cook it's up to me to make sure he creates good food. Shall try to summon up enough vitality to peek and peer and check everything in the house – it's such a bore!

Saturday 8th June – Rugger at the Sports Club. St George's Day. England win. Afterwards sundowners. We change at the Watsons'. She has a bird mind, much worse than me! She is totally concerned with trivialities. The stiffening to her dress, her young son's wakefulness, shaving the armpits ... to us, complete strangers. And he, with his beaky nose and chin – a typical 'northern' canny look. In the car she hides her face because she was in an accident and P's driving unnerves her. (It wasn't half as wild as usual!) Went to the City Bar, had mussel spaghetti – delicious! P and Ken play the fool, tapping out tunes on glasses. The sitting at a table nearby follow suit and start bashing their plates ... it can't be much fun running a restaurant with rugger types around. We go on to the dance. Have a terrific argument with a South African from Kilembe Mines about Emmanuel Velikovsky's theories about cosmic origins in his book 'Worlds in Collision'. He is enormously tall, like most SA rugger types, a palaeontologist and geologist. Later we discover we were talking about different books – he meant 'When Worlds Collide'.

When rock and roll starts up I have an exhausting time, pairing up with all the odds and sods who think they can dance. Jean Mackay sits and mopes because Bob spends his time with 'the boys' at the bar – what does she expect? I've learnt to accept that sort of thing. Do an old-fashioned waltz with the geologist. Harry Harbottle goes to sleep as usual. We serenade him, he's very drunk, they drape a St George's flag around him and balance a tray on his head. P is about to squirt a fire extinguisher at him, when he wakes up and says, 'I know what you're talking about,' which is very funny. After more ribbing he slowly exits, dignified-like with the strains of 'Why was he born so beautiful' wafting after him. His wife Moira had already gone home without him. On the way to the Tabaris' we stop, with dirt in the choke, so Steve stays the night with us.

Sunday 9th June – Fergus 4 months today. The Griffiths over for tea. Tea with the Gortons in the afternoon. Dorothy has heard that the Griffiths 'hot it up' as she put it, so she doesn't want to meet them. I think they're very nice. She gives me a theatrical make-up box that belonged to her brother, it's full of sticks of grease paint, fake jewellery, false hair, spirit glue etc, very sweet of her.

Monday 10th June – Hugh gives a party for Bolster, a director of the Uganda Co. The Hassals and the Bettis are there. Mrs Betti is Polish: 'Hai daunt knauw'. She's dour, shy, sits with her feet pointed in like a little girl. Francis asks us back for drinks afterwards. We had brought Rowland with us in the Volksie, and we start up, ostensibly to go home, as we don't want Bolster to join us, but he is discovered hanging onto the back trying to stop us, he must have been tight. Standing there in the moonlight the ground seems to shiver, I wonder if an earthquake is about to start, but its safari ants, they are under the dry leaves on the driveway, and all shiver at once – most uncanny.

Sunday 16th June – We see some of the Gortons' films re coffee planting and their various travels. Develops into a gay party. Hugh is there. We discuss the 'Worlds in Collision' theories, and Hugh poses the question, 'If the population is increasing, and everyone has a soul, where do all the extra souls come from?' If it's a matter of reincarnation ... well, no one has the answer to that, as we don't know enough about it. Inevitably the war is discussed. They were all in it. Francis was a prisoner of war with the Japs. Would we have won it without the Americans? P says we could have done, the others the opposite. I say nothing as I have no idea. I do say I disliked Dulles's letterbox mouth, soapbox self-righteousness and despised Ike's watery personality.

Tuesday 18th June – Go shopping. Jean Mackay admits she's pregnant. P was right. P goes on rugby tour – Nairobi–Arusha–Nakuru. Lovely feeling of freedom!

Friday 21st June – P phones, has had an interview with Geo. Williamson and Co., says it's very promising. He has to write again in September. He's met Alistair Prescott, his old friend, and informs him that he is one of Fergus's godparents! Strangely enough, I'm beginning to miss him ... Sat and Sun, drinks with Hugh and the Griffiths.

Tuesday 25th June – Arrives back lateish. We discuss my going home. He convinces me it's an impossibility, this year at any rate. Mummy and Daddy have offered to pay my fare, but he points out that we would have to pay them back. He made it plain that harping on about returning home upsets him. It's the first time we've been away from each other for so long, and it's done us both good. All's well between us now, hope it lasts. If only we two can be happy together, I don't mind how many endless sweltering years pass before seeing my dear family.

Saturday 29th June – Rugby, Kampala v Nile at Nakivubu Stadium. We win.

Drinks at the Police Club. Chat to Mike Kagwa, such an intelligent, well-brought-up young man. He was adopted by an English family, went to a good public school, and is better read than most Englishmen. He also plays rugby very well. Meal at the City Bar. Jane sleeps over at the Mackays', on the couch. The ayah was there. A risky experiment, but it worked, this time.

Sunday 30th June – Mackays, Lanes, Steve G. and Ted Seed all go to Entebbe. Females swim and sunbathe, males swim and play golf. Jane has her first proper meal in an hotel – sits on two cushions and wields an outsize spoon. Tries to attract the attention of various small children at nearby table by shouting 'Yah' very loudly! Otherwise very well behaved. She doesn't throw her plate on the floor or try to get down. She wears only a hat and a smile at the pool. I get rather sunburnt.

Thursday 4th July – See *Moby Dick*. Well acted, with authentic settings. P said parts of it bored him.

Saturday 6th July – He goes to Kitale. I have drinks with the Griffiths. Tremendous arguments about the modern playwrights, Tennessee Williams particularly. They say they only go to the theatre to be entertained, to laugh, not to think, because they've been through a war, seen enough misery, and that daily life is sordid. My generation feel they have missed out on something, they seek it in their writings. I tried to point out that these writers are trying to express something of intrinsic value, not just digging up sex for the sake of 'épater les bourgeois'. Williams's people are mainly inarticulate, tragic, doomed. I instanced *Hamlet*, there you have sex, incest, murder – laid on with a trowel! They agree it's a worthy classic, but not of our time. I say the plays of our time are stark and match the utilitarian age, someone has to speak for the lonely, weak ones. Just because Francis has been a prisoner doesn't remove all responsibility for the fate of the rest of humanity. They then said that playwrights write for money, and that a coterie play seen by only a handful of people is not worth writing.

Sunday 7th July – P comes back in the afternoon, Alberto doesn't turn up, it's the ayah and the toto's half day. There's no light in the kitchen – Life!

Tuesday 9th July – Fergus is five months today. Put the children in the same room, see if it works.

Wednesday 10th July – It doesn't – yells all round! F has a tooth just peeping through. I'd better wean him quickly! He's having Farex twice a day, and bone and veg broth at 2 pm. P has been put in charge of Luga Division.

Thursday 11th July – P goes in shopping. I go over to the Griffiths to borrow their playpen for the trip to Kitale. Jean and I go over to Hugh's for a while, quite fun, H is amiable. In the evening we see a red planet, at least Jean and Francis do, I thought it was a plane, it moves a bit then disappears. We don't hear the sound of a plane ... Had a terrific lambasting from them both, 'Shouldn't let P go off for all these odd weeks and weekends, but should make the interest at home'. They said they had seen so many lousy marriages, where the husband felt he must be 'out with the boys', long after he's too old to keep up with them and drinking too much as a result. I tried to stand up for P, that he felt loyalty to the club, and wouldn't let them down over a touring fixture, and that I also enjoyed the game and the social side. He'd promised to give it up after this season. I admitted I wished he had discussed it with me before telling the organisers that I wasn't coming ... I could do with some leave ... then Jean and I got into a huddle, and we decided I must show more love, it's there, but I don't show it enough. He probably thinks I care more for the children and my separate needs. She runs me home in the car. P arrives. She's had a few whiskies and is quite whoozy, so she lashes into him about integrity, putting one's utmost time and energy into one's job, even if you don't enjoy working within certain limitations.

Friday 12th July – The curse – thank God! I write to Mummy. Jean comes over for coffee.

Saturday 20th July – Game at Nsambya. P is picked to play for Uganda against a Combined Universities team. Has been invited to play for a virtual East African side at Eldoret on 7th, but he may not be able to get away. The Boshoffs are back, glowing with health! Jane is with us, more than holding her own amongst the older children. Next day Boshoffs come to lunch, plus the Griffiths and their children. One of the pleasantest days for a long time. Jean and Mireille seem to have something in common which gives me great pleasure. In the evening we go over to the Gs', Jean sinks quite a few whiskies.

Monday 22nd July – Jean in bed with a suspected miscarriage. If I'd known she was pregnant I'd have asked P to ease up on the drinks ... she also cleaned Sir Clutha Mackenzie's car yesterday (their boss). Silly creature, apparently she really wants the baby, funny way to go about it, excess booze and strenuous exercise? Tuesday and Wednesday, each day have gone over to see her. She fears F has an inherited liking for the bottle, and may end up like his father, who died of the same. The other day P and Rowland were judging shambas at the Blind School, and said F had had quite a few bottles of beer in his desk, and had evidently stocked up before they arrived. Poor Jean, they had this problem before they arrived in Uganda, and they conquered it together. It was when he was worrying about their coffee farm at Kiambu in Kenya. But they sold it. I gather they are fairly well-off, wonder what is worrying him now?

Thursday 25th July – Jean in the European Hospital, may have to have an operation. P goes to see her. Letters from M and Nan. Freddy Gorton came over to see me for a while. He is so frail, I'm afraid he'll just crumble up one of these days.

Saturday 27th July – Jean still in hospital, I was going to go to the rugger match, but then F came over with their two children and asked me to look after them. It's the official opening of the Blind School, and he'll be extremely busy, so I offered to take them down with me later.

Sunday 28th July – P arrives back at 11 am this morning. This is too much for me, having waited anxiously all night, not knowing if he's had an accident! I can't bear it any longer, we have a row. He thinks he can just breeze in, 'Sorry I'm late darling', as if it's all in order. I go for a walk to try and dissipate my frustration. The van swishes past, I think he's gone off to Kampala again. I just dissolve into tears. My walk has taken me towards the Bettesons' house, and their car comes past just as I've turned back towards home ... I'm forced to exchange greetings with my give-away wet face. In the evening P and I have a serious talk. The upshot is he agrees to try and be back by midnight when he's out on a bachelor evening, but he says he can't promise ... rather funny, when I say he might have been with another woman he says the only woman he talked to was Moira Harbottle, and I could hardly be jealous of her!

Tuesday 30th July – See *Anastasia* with Ingrid Bergman, very good. Letter from Freda Evans, enclosing a cutting of Dik and Shirley at his wedding – gives me a twinge.

Thursday 1st August – Cocktail party at the Town Hall. Great fun. I wear my new black hat, with a red rose on one side, an unusual extravagance! Later we, and the Combined Universities side eat at the City Bar. Much horseplay by the visitors. My lovely new hat is stolen out of the car ... taken as a souvenir no doubt. One of the team, John, looks like a Greek god, shortish, but with fantastic thighs! He's very conceited though.

Saturday 3rd August – Terrific game, they won 62 – 9! I wore a slim sheath of pink shantung, made from the material Mummy sent me. Bit of a clash with my yellow straw hat, but had no other since my new one was stolen. Fergus was relatively quiet, stuck in the manager's office, but Jane definitely made her mark on the proceedings … the Uganda Police band had struck up before the game, and she strolled out of the stands and walked slowly down the row, inspecting each one solemnly, then a police bod picked her up and brought her back to me amid clapping. I blushed puce! She was completely unperturbed! Later on the noise and boredom made her tearful, and I was glad when it ended. P strained a muscle in his leg, and was limping after the game.

Changed and dined at Col. Gordons', leaving Jane upstairs with the ayah, and Fergus in the Col's bedroom. I had a sore throat and he offered me Benzole Expectorant, with a sly leer, saying it had a delayed action effect…? Nicky Holcombe, a blue-rinsed female, who seemed to have a husband in Legco [Legislative Assembly] was his partner. Animated discussion of 'Cohenism' – I requested a definition. He said, 'Like the welfare State.' [Sir Andrew Cohen was the then Governor of Uganda for the Labour government.] He gave an example of it: When the Rugby Union sent out a team to tour Kenya and Tanganyika it cost next to nothing, as they went in their own cars and stayed in private homes – private enterprise. When the Soccer Union sent a team to Dar-Es-Salaam, it cost £10,000. They flew there and back and stayed in hotels – the bill was subsidised by the government. While dining I began to feel sleepy, courtesy of cough mixture. Nicky talked about the new Aga Khan, how she had met Aly and Sadruddin when they were youngsters, and said, 'This Prince Kerim, he's quite a catch!' Her rolling eyes hinted that she would have liked to do the fishing herself!

The dance and barbecue was held at the Top Club. I usually hate these informal dances, you can't dress up and look your best, but have to dress casually. Richard Todd the film star was there, he'd been filming locally, much shorter than I imagined. He was chatting to Peter Robbins the Rugby International. I danced quite a lot and enjoyed myself. P propped up the bar most of the evening talking to Gordon's secretary. Three of the undergraduates put on an impromptu cabaret, singing calypsos, including 'Don't Touch me Nylons', with guitars. Someone shouted, 'Can't we have some clean ones?' So then they sang 'The Hole in the Elephant's Bottom!' We broke up regretfully at 4 am. Thereafter things took a turn for the worse. P was carrying

Jane downstairs, slipped, fell, and Jane's ankle was twisted, but we didn't realise it then ... he was full of booze, and had a strained leg.

The engine stalled halfway between Mukono and home – we had to sit and doze until daytime. By this time Jane was yelling with pain, Fergus woke up and demanded his food! Chaos! P looked at the engine, fiddled around with my nail file, and at last got it going. Needless to say we had a terrible row, his hangover worsening as time went on.

Sunday 4th August – Slept late. P supposed to play an epic game of golf with Peter Robbins, Currie and Bob, downing a pint of beer before each hole, but in the event he drove into Entebbe in the afternoon and watched cricket. We realised poor Jane had hurt her ankle, and put cold compresses on it.

Saturday 17th August – Butch hasn't eaten his supper. Most unusual. I start the symptoms of mumps.

Sunday 18th August – Butch is given a tick fever injection. He keels over afterwards, his mouth and eyes are jaundiced. The Lanes come over, they're going to buy a puppy from the Griffiths.

Monday 19th August – Butch is in a bad way, we bring him into the bedroom. We could hear his heart beating from another room. He is such a wonderful friend, gay and puppylike, and now lies supine on the carpet, his breath laboured, his body cold. His fur stands on end. At lunch the toto brings my tray (am in bed with mumps), when he opens the door Butch streaks out – we think he must be better, P follows him out. Butch dies in the sun. Now am told boxers have weak hearts, and the injection was too much for him.

Tuesday 27th August – All this month Grey and Jean have been gossiping about P, how badly he treats me, coming home late all the time etc ... This evening Grey appears, he knows P has gone shopping. Had just got out the bath, dog-tired after a hard day, have been wearing binders and taking Epsom's Salts to stop the milk. Fergus doesn't like it very much, but is being very good on the whole. Grey lashes right into me: I'm too loyal, I must show P where he goes wrong for the sake of myself and the children … he gives me the impression that P's work is not up to standard, that the Uganda Co. is fed up with waiting for him to make up his mind whether to leave or not, and that we would be in Queer St pretty soon. Everyone on the estate thinks I should stand up to him.

I'm muddled and bewildered by this stream of opinionated argument. I've only Grey's word about P's work standard, and the Uganda Co.'s attitude. Grey repeats to me things that I've told Jean in the strictest confidence. He makes me feel that I haven't been doing my duty. She was a necessary safety valve at the time of his tour, when I was so lonely and depressed. I've already told P that his lack of affection, no sex, and always staying away in the evenings is making my life a misery.

Then he tries to make love to me, swearing that, 'You are so desirable, if I was free I'd marry you tomorrow!' Fortunately P comes back before Grey can do any physical damage. Grey starts on him, so I go to bed. I wake up later, they're still talking far into the night.

Wednesday 28th August – Jean comes over. She apparently gave P some 'good advice' at the Bettesons' birthday party on Saturday. I'm sick to death of their interference. I tell Jean that I don't want the Blandy marriage to be a subject of conversation in future, it's taboo! In the evening I fed Fergus, then faced up to P. I tell him I don't care how lazy, conceited, and selfish he is, how bad at his work, we are in this together, and even if he's mistaken with the Kenya gamble, I can always get a job as I did before. [Tea planters' wives were not allowed to work.] All I ask is that he shows me some respect, be given a chance to be an equal partner in the marriage, not just a 'yes' woman. He agreed to this and was visibly cheered up. I admitted one of my faults was talking too much. How I regret opening up to Jean … although it did just about save my sanity!

Thursday 29th August – P gives me a £5 cheque and his love. I feel happier since we had it out. Mummy sends me a 20-bob PO, very kind of her. Sapple has suggested trying the Nandi job. P has arranged for us to go there this Sat after the seven-a-side rugby match. Big muddle over who will look after Jane while we are away. In the end the Bettesons take her, with an ill grace.

Saturday 31st August – Nandi is a beautiful place, with rounded volcanic hills, and a lake in the distance. That's the view from our house-to-be. It's an invigorating climate, with plenty of rain. The manager, Douglas Taylor, and his little dark wife Midge have one rather spoilt daughter. They are a pleasant couple, he's in his fifties, she's a good deal younger. Their house is a huge, timber-ceilinged place, the garden is impressive, with pergolas, rockeries, and pedestals dotted around. Stately trees surround a beautiful lawn. P likes the look of the tea, and of the factory, and Taylor's attitude to his staff.

I'm most impressed with our house – no bigger than at Salama, but it's well planned. Lovely brick fireplace, parquet floors, airing cupboards, new fridge, Rayburn stove, a store that locks up. The garden is full of flowers, excellent Swazi grass lawn, vegetable patch, and fruit trees. The Nandi Bears Club is nearby, with golf, tennis, cricket, squash courts. Eldoret is the nearest shopping centre, 40 miles.

September – Not motivated to fill in diary. Can't wait to leave here. It's very hot. I only see the Griffiths once more, at Colin's b'day party. Skating on thin ice all afternooon. Either false bonhomie or chilly silences. P has an awful time with Grey, he told him never to come to our house again after one more blazing row. Now he is Acting Manager, it's gone to his head, and he gets at P at every opportunity. Jean had her baby on the 3rd.

Friday 4th October – We are going to the coast for a few days – joy!

Sunday 6th October – Last tea with the Gortons, such a sweet couple … I'll miss them.

The trip to the coast in our little Volkswagen was fun! We stayed one night at the Norfolk Hotel in Nairobi, then carried on the next day to Malindi.We spent the next night on the road, and waking up in the car and watching a yellow turning to palest blue dawn, with the acrid smell of mysterious herbs, khaki grass, and dust, was a precious and unforgettable experience. The Tsavo Game Park had wonderful baobab trees, 'upside down trees' as they are called because of the fat trunks and spindly branches. Elephants loomed ahead on the road, as well as rhinos.

The night we arrived at the Kikambala Hotel, hot and grubby from the trip, with two wailing children, we were magically soothed by the sight of a tall waiter in kanzu, fez, waistcoat and cummerbund, summoning guests to dinner with a kind of triangle gong, soft melodious sounds over and over like a lullaby. Palm trees bent over against the full moon, lagoon waters licked quietly at the white sand, and we settled gratefully into our little palm-roofed chalet, lit by an oil lamp.

It was just what our frayed nerves needed. We spent two weeks lolling around on the sand, or swimming in the calm waters. Fergus and Jane loved it. The food was great, but sometimes we went out to the Blue Marlin Hotel for a meal or a drink, they served a superb kedgeree. We met a deep-sea diver, Ian, who told us tales of an underwater cave where he swam and stroked tame giant groupers. We heard later that he'd hit his head on a rock and become paralysed, and had to be flown to Stoke Mandeville.

On 16th December we were invited to a dinner party in our honour, to meet the other members of staff at Nandi Tea Estates. If only we could have known ... but one never does. The first omen was the ayah falling ill. She didn't come to work that day. Fergus had a slight cold, but nothing serious. He was too young for a dressing gown, but he had on a nappy, nightie, and two shawls pinned around him, Jane had on her pyjamas and dressing gown. Because of the threat of Mau Mau attacks we never left the children at home – no one did. We had a specially made mattress that fitted in the back of the Volksie when the seat back was taken out. We then stuffed the small space behind the seats with cushions.

The two children went off to sleep as we drove to the Taylors' house. Next warning, our battery was a bit flat, so P parked on a slightly downward slope so we could take off again later. Then, because of the ornamental rockeries around the house, we had to park some little distance away. Normally the ayah would sit in the front seat with them and doze off. The dinner went with a swing, good food and plenty of wine. It was such a change for me to be surrounded by intelligent, witty people who weren't half sozzled, people who actually listened to what one had to say, that I lost track of time. At one stage Midge said, 'Shouldn't you check up on the children?' To my eternal shame, not wanting to rock the boat, I said, 'I'm sure they're fine.' After a while I asked P to go and have a look at them, so he went out. He came back and said they were OK. He listened, heard no sound, but he didn't look inside the car.

About 11 pm we finally said goodnight to everyone, and stumbled past the rockery in the dark to the car. I opened the door; the light came on. Jane was sleeping peacefully, but Fergus had slipped down into the cushions behind the seats, head down. He was cold. I held him to me as we rushed back into the house. He was laid on the dining room table and P tried CPR, mouth-to-mouth breathing, trying to pump air into his little chest ... he looked so beautiful in his white nightie, a little angel. Eventually we had to accept that he was dead.

Doug Taylor was influential in the district, and he quashed any idea of legal intervention. There was a post mortem. They agreed it was an accident. The coroner said fluid from Fergus's cold had drowned him when he slid upside down. I breast fed him for 5 months, he was the happiest, calmest darling, such a sunny nature – and he died needlessly at 11 months. I'm so glad we had had him christened. I don't ever want to forget him. I'll *never* forgive myself for not going to check on them, and I'll *never* forgive P for neglecting to look when he did go. There was a simple funeral service. Fergus is buried in the churchyard at Nandi Hills. Such a small white coffin.

I was totally distraught for weeks. Poor Jane must have wondered what had happened to her little brother. But she was only 18 months old herself. I would wake up in the middle of the night and suddenly remember, scream out in horror, sob for hours. P never showed any emotion. Stiff upper lip and all that. I suppose bombing Hamburg hardened him – what is the death of one little baby compared to killing thousands...

P got very impatient with me: 'Pull yourself together!' I thought about the idyllic time we'd spent at the coast, when we had gone deep sea fishing. I was the only one to catch something, it felt pretty big, we struggled to haul it on board, then one of the crew said, 'It's a shark!' They cut my line. Another day we found a huge iguana, like an ancient dragon ... Fergus got prickly heat, we lazed under the palm trees, he was fascinated by the hotel dog, who came and sat on our rug ... if only we could turn back time. I had had more love from my baby son than ever from my husband. He never made love to me once, even though we were supposed to be close again.

Mummy came over to stay with us. She was wonderful with Jane, told her stories, played with her, but she and P quarrelled incessantly, she never kept quiet if she saw injustice on his part. It pulled me out of my grief-stricken daze, trying to keep the peace between them.

To Fergus   Nandi Hills 1957

    Unnaturally we animate stairways
    Flat slab stones echo hollow to our feet.
    Men in black carry a box
    Their solemn uneven tread
    Pretend it's heavy, like a play.
    All different heights – pantomime of death
    So many bearing one so small and cold.
    Eleven months of this our life
    And ours the guilt – 'If only'...
    For now our nerves are tingling, sharp
    Anguish slides below the carapace of habit
    Black gulfs yawn, unreal sea-tasting
    Sad self loss; to save our reason
    Lose the cause, numbed nerve reject.
    All of time to ease the shock
    Deaden pain, provide excuses...

1958

23rd January 1958 – Had a tiff over Peter Pillbrow. [He was a charming and cultured golfer who had dared to talk to me like a human being. The rest of them avoided us as though our misfortune might contaminate them.] In the car going home he's slanging me as usual, but Mummy, sitting in the back, pipes up and starts on about our ancestors being as good as his. I cringe with embarrassment. The other night he didn't come back for tea or supper, and I'm frantic with worry. Does that mean I must love him? He'd said soon after Fergus died that we must live together without bitterness or self-pity, and that if I went back to UK he could not go on without me ... but he shows me no love

Saturday 25th January – Go to Sholto Douglas's farewell party. Very well attended. Jane sleeps in the car. Mrs Matson of the beady eyes asks me if I will help with the cricket lunch on Sunday. I dance with Skinner, he's attractively withdrawn, with a nice sense of humour. Matson gives a sentimental speech. Mummy gets rather bored and we leave early (for us) 2 am!

Sunday 26th January – Go to church. Our Jane and Jane Taylor wander in and out with each other's shoes on. P has to go out after them. Drinks at the Club. M and Mrs Outram have a natter about 'the good old days'. Bill Williams comes back to lunch.

Tues 28th January – Going down quite a small step in a friend's garden, Jane falls and breaks her collarbone. She's in a lot of pain. We take her to Dr Rhote in Kaimosi. She gave him her right hand to shake, he couldn't believe she'd broken it, but the x-ray proved it. Said she was too young to be put in plaster, so he operated, drilling a hole in the two bones, and joining them with copper wire. I stayed overnight in the hospital with her. She was awake but dazed, groaning sometimes. Guilt and loss flooded back. I'm afraid she'll hurt the wound, she thrashes about so. Her arm is strapped too tightly to her side. Letter from Pat, she may be getting married again, to Mike Hill. Nan is in Germany now.

Saturday 1st February – Jane is better, I've taken off her bandage.

Sunday 2nd February – M looks after Jane at home, as she might fall if she plays with other children. Just before we leave P and M have a stinking row! Shouting in the garden. In spite of that we have an enjoyable day at the Club. I play lots of tennis, P cricket in spite of a sprained ankle, 24 runs in 15 mins.

Have big conference with Matson and Ken Archer about starting up a dramatic club. Matson praises P's cricketing ability. P and I seem to have reached an unspoken understanding – he is mine again. My rebellious thoughts of leaving him fall away as soon as he seems to want me again ... if he really cares about me, I'd be loth to leave here, the life is so pleasant, and healthy for Jane.

Tuesday 4th February – Take Jane to Kaimosi to have the stitches out. The Sister yanks them out. Too soon, it turns out, as the stitches 'run' and she's left with a permanent scar. Afterwards have tea with Dr Green and his wife. Jane plays with their son, M and P maintain a hostile silence.

Saturday 11th February – Farewell for Midge Taylor, who's going on holiday to her family in Australia. Welcome to a new couple, the Potters. They're nice.

Monday 17th February – Drinks with Doug Taylor, Dr Eden is there. We hear M is due to go back to UK tomorrow, her three-month return ticket expires. None of us want her to stay, it's been a harrowing time, being a buffer.

Tuesday 18th February – Take her to New Lincoln Hotel in Eldoret. She makes a god-awful fuss when she discovers the bus is multi-racial! There is a separate compartment for her. I do sympathise with her up to a point, with her be-ringed fingers and large amount of luggage, she might be a temptation to thieves ... you'd think her compassion for the downtrodden Africans, as evinced in our many political arguments, would make her glad to be thrown in amongst them! She even darts out of the hotel and harangues departing white drivers to let her travel with them to Nairobi ... shaming. P's opinion of her sinks even lower.

Wednesday 19th February – Women's League meeting. I try to canvas actors for our drama club. Go for a longish walk in the woods above David de la Hay's house. [He was our young assistant.] Exhilarating!

Friday 21st February – Letter from M. She quite enjoyed her trip in the bus, but had the usual urges and couldn't make the driver understand ... that must have been funny. M, with all her coy, genteel euphemisms. I should have told her to ask for the 'choo'. P and I felt a distinct sense of relief after she left – what trouble a well-meaning mother-in-law can stir up. As a catalyst she helped to wake me up from my stupor of self-pity, encouraged me to paint again, start the drama society. And she was very good with Jane.

Saturday 23rd February – Jane's nose worse, looks like impetigo. Now she's got a bad cold. I decide not to go to Turbo with P. (Funny name, reminds me of dark toiling turbines and turbid toads ...) P makes 54 runs.

Monday 24th February – See Dr McNight at Kapsabet. Write to Mr and Mrs Gault.

Wednesday 26th February – Jane a little better. We dine with the Croxfords. She's a very pleasant girl, but withdrawn. I'm told she was married before, but left her husband after a month. She never drinks alcohol.

Saturday 1st March – We play tennis with Taylor and Viner. See 'A Town Like Alice'. Very good film. Too much death and despair. When Virginia McKenna finally meets up with her man after believing him dead, and she has carried the little blond baby all the way through the jungle, something broke inside me and I had to go outside and weep. Oh that my son could have only seemed to be dead, and had lived. P comes out looking for me. He says it's no good giving in, and we are going to be reminded of him many times in the future. I go back to the club, swollen-eyed.

Finlay Campbell stays the night. Fantastic man. Hugs a bottle of whisky to his breast all the time. He built a large three-storeyed house with a verandah running all the way round the top storey. That way he could survey the whole of his farm, with a telescope in one hand and the whisky in the other. Any malingerers were shouted at; his lung power was considerable. One day the old tar-clogged stove set fire to the chimney. He threw all his clothes out of the window, while a crowd of his labour (mostly illegal squatters) watched below. By the time he'd reached the ground all the clothes had vanished! His servant was trying to haul out the furniture. 'Don't bother with that,' he yelled, 'Save the whisky!' His house fell about his ears as he tried to rescue his precious liquor cabinet.

Sunday 2nd March – Kakamega team here for cricket. P makes 11. We get a walkover in the tennis competition. We draw with the Grants. I get all my serves over the net, but P poaches every single return. Most embarrassing, as we win a cup.

Friday 7th March – Dinner with the Grants. They have some wonderful jazz records. Their child, Lyn, wanders in and out all unheeded all evening. She wears a differant outfit each time, sports a large white bow on her head. She'll either be very brainy or totally impossible or both!

Monday 10th March – Croxfords to dinner. Jill tells me Peter Pillbrow's wife is in hospital – completely paralysed. Jill has been asked to tell him, by friends of his wife … but she is wary of telling him, not knowing if they are separated, or estranged.

Wednesday 12th March – We play the Bevans, from Sirocco. I think my serve is improving since P told me to cut out the frills. Meeting of the Kenya Women's League. The president, Mrs Anderson, is rather depressing about the probable resurgence of Mau Mau activity. I suppose she's right. She has a mat of dark hair above a low brow, piercing blue eyes in a dead-white face. I talk to Peter Pillbrow. I don't tell him about his wife, feel it's none of my business, but feel guilty not doing so, what if she is lying in agony, waiting for him to call?

Thursday 20th March – Peter and Joan Wright to dinner. He gets a bit glassy-eyed. They discuss P's idea of withering tea by sound waves. Peter W thinks tea should be packed in polythene bags instead of clumsy and expensive tea chests. He says they are all die-hards in Nandi and won't change anything. They knew young Hugh Halliday's parents, they are gentle people, doesn't understand why H is so gauche. Blames boarding school.

Saturday 22nd March – P goes to the TRI Conference in Kericho. Meets Holmes of Brooke Bonds, the boss, whom he knew in India. He was most effusive and said we must come and stay with him any time. He also met Rose, our successor at Salama, Chavasse and Johnny Boyle. Decorations at our cricket dance include crossed bats surmounted by a cricket box! Have to sell raffle tickets so miss supper. Play Jockeys and Horses. I am P's horse, but right-handed, left hand weak from too much tennis and polio, so I don't do very well. Allan Moore, who is sixty-something, tries to kiss me when the lights go out. Lots of things auctioned in aid of the John Collins Memorial Pavilion.

Sunday 23rd March – Nandi v Kipkabus. We win, P scores 90. Simon Rowan and Peter Streeton are amusing, and bawdy, on the pitch and in the pavilion! Both very hung over from the dance. In the evening the KAR (King's African Rifles) bods set up a stall with a bazooka on display, a walkie-talkie radio, photos of the 'wild men' who track down the Mau Mau to their lairs. I ask them if they could lend me a tin opener to open Jane's tin of beans, but they hadn't got one, Modern Army – huh! They don't manage to recruit P, but do get some of the youngsters to 'take the Queen's shilling'. One of the KAR boys was in Germany recently, so we sing some nostalgic German songs. I talk to a farmer from Songhor; he looks most fetching in his 'blues'. We discuss which is the most important sense.

I say the sense of touch, he says if you can't see or hear you might as well be dead.

Friday 28th March – Take Jane over to the McWilliams in the morning. After lunch we set off for Kampala. P is to play for Eldoret. Takes 4 hours. The road has improved and we don't stop for food. We stay with the Boshoffs. We beat Harlequins 27–10.

Saturday 29th March – Kampala beat Eldoret, very good game. P and I stooged around town in the morning. I bought Jane a toy wheelbarrow and a baby suitcase, also a pincushion-type flower holder and a bra. While buying the latter the saleswoman was staring fixedly at my bronzy pink earrings – it seems she has a necklace exactly the same shade and has never been able to match it ... so I gave her mine and she gave me a white pair in exchange! We see Joan Tyler, who's now running the flower shop next to Drapers, how that woman works! See all the old faces again. Laurie Laurier with his pretty pregnant wife, he whispers that they are off to a jazz club in Jinja, of all places. Ted Seed comes up, all smiles, he's no longer engaged. Great thrill when Harry Harbottle climbs onto the bar, to the strains of 'Why was he born so beautiful'. He prays for silence, then presents P with a farewell gift, a silver barrel-shaped tankard with his name inscribed on it. They demanded a speech and P gave a few well-chosen words. Mireille Boshoff and I went off to Makerere College to see *A Doll's House* by Ibsen. The 'little squirrel' was well played, the set and clothes excellent. Went home soon after the play. P and his cronies were drinking in 'the Silver Springs' until the small hours.

Thursday 3rd April – Dinner with the Thompsons. They play Saint Saens' 'Animal Suite' poems recited by Noel Coward. We talk about Vandals and Goths. The needle Tommy sat on years before came out of his thigh recently!

Sunday 6th April – Cecilia Collie and Harris come to stay. Still prattles on in her determinedly vivacious way. Jane is lost in admiration of Harris and his grave and manly demeanour. We take them up to the club, Bob Taylor is rather struck with her.

Friday 11th April – Cecilia and Harris set off for Kitale, leaving us a huge bag of oranges from their orchard.

Saturday 12th April – Peter Williams' wedding. Jane is naughty and has to be led out. A beautiful disembodied voice rings out at the end of the service. At the reception I meet the owner – fat, greedy and very Northern Irish! I wear my old hat, covered in net so it looks new. It's at the Eldoret Club. We meet the Huttons – he sallow and slightly knobbly, she terribly thin but attractive in an Audrey Hepburnish way. Joy, the bride, is amazing – she made and iced the terrific wedding cake, and also made her wedding dress and going-away outfit. We waited for the Boshoffs to arrive from Uganda, they were late, so we went on to the Sports Club. By the time they did arrive the match had been cancelled ... there was another wedding reception going on there so we joined in! At least I was correctly dressed, with my hat – Mireille drove us and the children back home.

Wednesday 16th April – The Mackays arrive. Angus is an alert baby. Have a play reading of *The Dover Road* in the evening. Ken Archer reads Mr Latimer, David Hamilton – Leonard, Robin Outram – Frances Taylor Eustacia, I read Anne. Bob's car is stuck on the way home – David de la Hay and his ruddy drain!

Saturday 19th April – Mike Hammerton's wedding. Needless to say, we don't go.

Wednesday 23rd April – First rehearsal of *I Killed The Count*. Sally Darling comes to read Anne. She's pretty awful, may have to drop her. David Hamilton romps thru' doing a comedy turn, some of his inflexions are very funny and well timed. Robin Outram drops out.

Saturday 26th April – Rugger at Kitale, Jane comes with us. Stay with Benjy at Endebess. Ye olde thatched farmhouse, lovely little rose garden. Jane has to sleep in the car all night as there is no cot or bed for her. She seems quite happy when I go to her in the morning.

Sunday 27th April – Set off for Soy. The Gaults are a pleasant couple, with a beef and dairy farm. Jane adored Mr Gault, who swung her round his head and took her for a walk. Hanne had said that Mrs G was tiresome, but I think it's Hanne who was tiresome! Wonderful dinner, liver and bacon cooked with rice, followed by bananas cooked in brandy with brown sugar, on a chafing dish at the table. The liver concoction had fennel in it, tasted a little of carroway seed. There's quite a bad storm in the night, I get up to close the window, but bump into P's bed on the way. I can't open the mosquito netting on the window, so have to go back to bed, bumping into his bed on the way (the beds are very close together in a tiny room). Later on the rain is blowing in badly and wetting our clothes. I get up and bump his bed again in the dark, curses from P! Manage to open the netting in the dark and close the window ... finally get back into bed, wet and exhausted.

The diary is missing or destroyed for the rest of the year. At the end of April I realised that I was pregnant again. We were overjoyed when it was confirmed, it felt as though we'd been given another chance to redeem ourselves and somehow make up for Fergus's horrible accident. We were due for leave towards the end of the year, so I had to plan to have the baby in UK, as planes did not accept women over seven months pregnant. We left Nandi Tea Estates and joined Kapchorua Estates. It was better to be away from all the people and places that would remind me of it. Our new boss was a pleasant enough man, bit of a soak, but easy going.

One morning Jane and I came across a tiny thin snake on the lawn at Nandi; the houseboy said it was a poisonous one. It reminds me of a night in that house when the safari ants (siafu) invaded us. Fergus and Jane were in bed in their room, I woke up in the middle of the night to see a shivering mass on the carpet, lit by moonlight. I blinked, then I felt a sharp nip on my arm. I didn't want to step into them. Woke P, who bravely rushed barefoot through to the children. We wrapped them in blankets, took them out to the Volksie, and spent the rest of the night in it. In the morning the ants had gone. The house was bare of any insects, and a cooked chicken in the larder was picked clean. It's one way to clean the house ... The cook told us that the ants hate the smell of khaki bush weed (khakibos) and won't go through ash, as it clogs their breathing apparatus, so if we saw an army on the march towards us we should scatter those items all round the house. There is a story that a baby was left out in his pram and the ants ate him ... I can believe it.

The house at Kapchorua was an old one, wooden, built up on stilts against a hill, rather like a New Guinea longhouse. There was long grass all around, with only the odd patch of canna lilies to prove it had ever been cultivated. The whole estate was a bit run down, but it was a foothold to better things, as P had been promised an estate in Meru, in the Nyambenis, the foothills of Mt. Kenya. It would be virgin forest, so he would have to start from scratch.

I had been painting watercolour sketches during the year, as well as writing short stories and poems, and doing a correspondence course with the Regent Institute in London. A couple of my stories were published by the *Kenya Weekly News*, and I was interviewed in Nairobi by a producer at KABS (a radio station). Because I lived in the bundu (bush), it would be difficult for them to use me, so I suggested I wrote a series of talks that I could record, but nothing came of it at that stage. Michael McCabe and Tim Bungay were two very talented professional actors who worked for them, and who later moved to South Africa.

It must have been August when we flew to London in a Vickers Viscount, a much better trip than the outward one in 1955. P had arranged to tour with a cricket team, the Kongonis (named after a type of buck). Various Kenya and Uganda expatriates travelled around the south of England, playing the local talent on village greens. I especially loved the Dorset countryside. We stayed in Wales with P's parents for a while, visited Pat and Fran and Sally. We went with them to the zoo and Regent's Park, then he returned to Kenya. I stayed with my parents in Hampstead while waiting for the birth. I was booked into Queen Charlotte's Hospital in Hammersmith.

One awful night when I was eight months gone, my father tried to make love to my mother. He chased her screaming into the kitchen in her home-made parachute silk nightie. She said he was hurting her. (I think she must have had something wrong with her insides – she was only 58, it shouldn't have been a big deal otherwise.) This was nightmarish, their intimate life was nothing to do with me, they shouldn't even be doing it, they were *old*! Having lost Fergus I was determined that nothing would damage the expected baby. I picked up a carving knife and threatened my father, if he ever tried to force her again I would kill him! It had the desired effect; he slunk back to bed. He was relatively sober for the rest of our stay. I had always been afraid of him, especially when drunk, but some cave-woman instinct came to the fore that night! Fortunately Jane was asleep in the bedroom, she would have been terrified.

The day before Jane's third birthday I told her she might have a little brother or sister for her birthday. I had a glass of Blandy's Madeira before going to sleep. The pains started in the early hours of the morning, and an ambulance took me to Queen Charlotte's. So Jane had a wonderful present, a baby brother, Michael Fergus Peel, born at about 8 am on 23rd November. Everything was normal: he was 7¾ pounds. When they put him in my arms, and I saw his little blond head, fuzzy cream down like a duckling, so like Fergus when he was born, it broke my heart. I was ecstatically happy, and sad. It was lonely having no husband to share the joy. We had to get a rabbi to circumcise him, because the hospital refused to do it. I was sent out of the room, but Mummy was allowed in ... why? She made a big fuss, said it was terrible watching it! Once I was fit enough we flew back to Kenya.

Nandi

1960

The new job in Meru was now confirmed, but first we would take more leave at the coast. We travelled down in convoy with our friends Simon Rowan and Peter Streeton. They had a lady doctor with them. When we arrived at the bungalows on the beach near Malindi, during the unpacking process Jane ate a whole packet of Daraprim anti-malarial tablets that she found in the car. (They were not bitter-tasting, as was usual.) The doctor insisted she went to the nearest hospital to have her stomach pumped out ... what a start to the holiday!

Once she was declared out of danger we could start the business of engaging a servant and buying food. Vendors wandered along the beach selling fruit, vegetables, crayfish and prawns. Old Juma was the resident houseboy, he said. His duties were minimal, as the bungalow was just a lean-to with a verandah, so his cleaning duties were mainly sweeping the sand out with a brush broom, and building fires for cooking. Michael was nearly six months now, and he loved sitting in the tepid lagoon water, with one of my old sunhats tied under his chin. He was so fair he had to wear a t-shirt in the sun. Jane loved playing in the fine white sand. There were brilliant fish near the reef, so we went goggling. I nearly drowned in four feet of water, as the white ball on top of the snorkel fell off and a gush of sea water shot into my mouth. I tried to stand up, and couldn't get my bearings because of the flippers! The others never noticed my agonised splashings, but I tore off the goggles and managed to grab some air. Once on my back I could calm down, pretend nothing happened, and swim back to them.

We visited the haunted city of Gedi. The legend has it that its founders were refugees from Malindi, who fled when Mombasa staged a punitive raid on them for aiding Portuguese attempts to capture the coast. Galla tribesmen later swept down from Somalia, ravaging several cities, but then they too abandoned it. For a while it was a centre of the gold and ivory trade. Then Arab slavers overran it in the sixteenth century, killing all the children and old people, and taking the able-bodied adults away with them. What's left of the stone buildings shows small rooms, very deep wells, shards, pots, dried-up fountains. The Friday mosque, with its tower, and the palace, are the only large buildings extant. It's surrounded by the dense, dark Sokoko forest, and is very cool. A charmed graveyard, alive with whispering spirits. I couldn't bear to be there at night. There's a small museum, containing porcelain from China, precious beads, some rusted weapons. The local people say it's haunted – even at midday the hushed coolness contrasts with the blazing heat elsewhere. It inspired my short story 'Yasmin', which was recorded by Colin Fish for the SABC.

Our doctor friend had to fly overseas, so the men of the party took her to Mombasa airport. When they came back next day, very much hung over, P wasn't with them. They had no idea what had happened to him. Simon Rowan said he would go back to look for him, I insisted on accompanying him, as I couldn't trust him not to go on another 'bender'. In Mombasa, after a fruitless morning searching the pubs and clubs, we stopped for a delicious curry at the Mombasa Club, overlooking Fort Jesus, the whitewashed stone prison in the harbour. After a couple of Pimm's, Simon went out again looking for P. No luck, so we drove back to Malindi. On the way he discovered I couldn't drive. He insisted on giving me a lesson, there and then. He encouraged me to go faster and faster, I steered while he worked the gears. Just past the Kalifi prison I saw a little Ford Prefect tootling along at about five miles per hour. Just beyond it was the ferry. 'Brake!' Simon yelled. I put my foot down. But it was the accelerator, not the brake. Realising that there was no way I could avoid smashing into the Ford I turned the wheel over to the left, and we capsized completely and landed upside down in the ditch.

Moments ticked by. There was a strong smell of petrol. The Customs officer started running up the road towards us. 'Quick,' Simon said, 'change places!' It's not easy changing places when you're upside down. Still we managed it in time to smile innocently at the mystified official. 'What happened?' he said in Swahili. Simon managed a technical explanation, which made no sense at all, but it was in kitchen Swahili, so he accepted that we were typical mad white settlers.

A chain gang of prisoners clanked past. Simon tried to enlist their help to pull us out of the ditch, but they demanded 300 shillingi, and we didn't have that much with us. He comandeered my new lipstick to fiddle around to see if there was a leak, or if it was just overspill? (It smelled of petrol ever after.) Just then a car with an Eldoret registration hove to. They kindly helped us pull the car back on the road, with the aid of a length of rope they happened to have in their boot. Amazingly the only damage was one punctured tyre.

When we arrived at the entrance to the bungalows, who should be standing there but Peter himself, furious, arms akimbo, demanding to know where the hell we had been. He well knew the adage, 'the best defence is attack'. We tried to explain that we had been looking for him. It turned out that he had been under a yellow 'Happy Taxi', trying to help the driver with a wheel that had fallen off, as we drove out to look for him. (I never did find out what he had been up to in Mombasa.) Glorious weather and long, lazy days slightly mollified his bad-tempered mood.

One particular day I manage to persuade him to come to bed for a bit of connubial bliss. He said all right then, but make sure you're protected. I put the diaphragm in all askew in my hurry – I mean, this was my once-a-year poke! It actually hurt, but I had to strike while the iron was hot. Months later, when I found out I was pregnant again, he said it couldn't be his child. I explained about the diaphragm, but he insisted that a surveyor name Dando must be the father. Dando was a very charismatic South African who had worked at Nandi Hills for a while, and had wowed all the local frustrated wives. He and I were friendly, but of course, nothing more. When Roger was born it was plainly obvious who the father was – a Peter clone if ever there was one. Still, for years he was convinced he had been cuckolded. It suited him to have more fuel for his resentment of me.

Sunday 20th March – We are packed up and set off for Meru. Stay the night at the Pig and Whistle. A rambling old wooden structure with great atmosphere. Guest houses up on stilts like Swiss chalets. Meet the manager and his wife, the Ambler-Davises.

Monday 21st March – Buy stores at Patel's duka. Go up to the estate.

Terrible road, potholed, but the most beautiful countryside. Lush forests, bracken everywhere, blackberries – could be in Cumberland!

Tuesday 22nd March – P goes to Nanyuki. In the afternoon we all go up to Nyambeni. Put up the tents. Dig a hole in the forest for the loo. Light a big fire for the bathwater. (Also to scare away the man-eating leopard reputed to haunt these parts.) Surround our large zinc bath with a roofless screen of poles interlaced with bracken. Have 2 tents, Jane and I in one, Peter and Michael in the other. That night there are 4 inches of rain. Tent roof implodes, go to huddle in P's tent the rest of the night. Next night we have 6 inches of rain! The labour build a thatched roof over the remaining tent. Spot glimpses of Mount Kenya between rain showers – it's so dramatic, black rocks, striped with snow. I try to paint it, many times, but we only see it free of cloud twice a year when the rains come.

Friday 25th March – Visit the Hattersleys at Kiega (the other side of the hill). He's a Methodist preacher, and his wife is a Yorkshire woman with a broad accent. She describes her daughter's hair as 'well mannered', said daughter cringes with embarrassment, but I think it's a delightful phrase!

Sunday 27th March – Go to Meru Club. Tea with the Bayles. He's the Assistant District Commissioner. Hodge is the DC. Jane makes her ghastly remark to Mrs Ambler-Davis. (No idea what it was, probably to do with her weight – first recorded incident of Jane's outspokenness!)

Saturday 15th April – East African Safari, we watch part of it, heavy going in the mud! Drinks at the Police Club afterwards, I feel sick [first mention of pregnancy].

Saturday 2nd May – Sent telegram to M. on her b'day (10th May) Meet Mr Gordon, the NBI supervisor at Mutheru. They don't want to risk their cars on our quagmired roads, so we leave them behind at Muthara. They are taken up to the estate. Very shaken up by the road, but think the countryside is wonderful.

145

Tuesday 17th May – Go to Nanyuki. Collect some of our stuff from storage in Meru on the way back. Spend most of the time with the Simons. Evening meal with Father Botta at the Kianjai Mission. He's a sweet little man, quite young. Very Italian, enthusiastic, organises lotteries to raise money for the struggling outpost. Hitches up his cassock, tucks it into his belt and plays soccer with his staff. Little white legs with red socks and football boots, incongruous!

Sunday 22nd May – Curry lunch at Police Mess, and a dance afterwards. Ken Brierly takes children. P plays squash.

Wednesday 27th May – Tony and Elaine Windus and Peter and Joan Wright come to lunch. In evening go to Pig and Whistle in Meru and dine with them.

Thursday 31st May – Go to Nairobi with Mr Patel the duka owner. Appt. with Mr Preston, the gynae. Stay with the Rand-Overys. They are very charming. Try to organise a recording with Alan Bobbe at KBC. Tea with Peter Wright.

Saturday 4th June – Meet Finlay Currie in Nanyuki. Children stay at the Brierlys'. Lunch with the Thompsons (he of the needle in his thigh).

Sunday 5th June – Stay with Mark Aitken. Rugger dance at the White Rhino. A boisterous crowd. We return late to pick up the children, and Mrs Brierly is very rude.

Tuesday 7th June – Barry Cliff, our new conservationist, comes to stay in our tent. We have moved into a long rondavel, which is actually two round ones joined together, with thatch on the roof to cut down on the heat. He climbs Mt. Kenya, says there's not much snow there now.

Saturday 11th June – Weekend stay with Geoff and Pat Cook. He's the D.O. at Nkubu. We take a camp bed and mattress. Tea with Mike Ardagh, a lean and humorous Irishman.

Sunday 12th June – Our anniversary. Very quiet. My play must have arrived at the *Kenya Weekly News* by now. Provincial Commissioner, Brig. Hughes, coming to lunch. He's very nice, asks us to stay with him any time we are in Nyeri (except for school hols!).

Friday 17th June – The Cooks come to stay. We walk up the stream to the old bomb crater. Has the most amazing undergrowth. Ferns, bracken. The children seem to fight a lot.

Sunday 19th June – The Ambler-Davises come to tea (owners of the P and W). The Cooks leave in the afternoon. My ayah is also having a baby – damn! Bad timing.

Thursday 30th June – Get McKinnon to take blood sample to take to Nairobi. Aggarwal makes a mess of the injection. Mrs Metchum will take it to N'bi.

Thursday 7th July – Victor Davis comes up to build our new house in the next valley. He's a Sikh in a turban. Strange name for a Sikh.

Sunday 10th July – I hear there are no antibodies in my blood.

Friday 15th July – The Jouberts come to lunch. They organised the original clearing of the forest, felling and towing away the giant trees. They lived in a caravan during that period, but have a home in Thompson's Falls. A really nice Afrikaans couple. Fond of Jane.

Sunday 17th July – Go to Nkubu Mission Hospital to arrange for birth of baby. Am examined by Sister Louisalba (Italian). I'll be staying with the Cooks until the birth.

Monday 18th July – Jack Coley comes to see about building new house.

Sunday 31st July – P takes me to Nkubu. My heart aches to see the children go with him at 6 pm, but there's no choice.

Monday 1st August – Baby due. Spend a pleasant day with the Cooks, an amusing couple.

Tuesday 2nd August – Go shopping in Meru with Patricia, Say goodbye to the Hodges (D.C. going on leave). Slight pains. After lunch go in to hospital. Take castor oil at 12.15 pm. Pains start in earnest at teatime.

Wednesday 3rd August – Roger born at 8.30 in evening after four hours labour. Poor lamb, he's only 5½ pounds. It's because I'm so active. Sister Louisalba says it's lucky he's small, because he was born face upwards. P and children come over and we toast Roger in champagne.

Friday 12th August – Leave hospital. The nuns were wonderful! Stay with the Cooks.

Saturday 13th August – Dinner with the directors at the P and W. Great fun.

Friday 26th August – Leave children with the Cooks. Spend the night at Embu with Peter Brown (Acting D.C.). Meet Lawrence Durrell's brother, Gerald. He's shortish, square, with a big pink face. Wears a safari suit. We talk a lot, mainly about animals (I think he wrote 'My Family and Other Animals' after this).

Saturday 27th August – Travel to Nairobi, stay at Norfolk Hotel. P plays squash.

Sunday 28th August – Meet the Wrights at Nairobi Club. I rest in afternoon, P watches cricket. Drinks with Otto in evening.

Monday 29th August – My b'day. Shopping. Leave Roger at the Lady Northey Nursing Home. Dinner with Jon Gordon (NBI). Roger's in a bedroom but he wakes up, all very awkward. Lovely old home.

Thursday 1st September – Drive back via Nkubu. Pick up Jane and Michael. Tea at P and W. P drives back to Meru for cement.

Wednesday 14th September – Tea at Maua with the Websters. They've replaced the Meagers. When we returned, our furniture had arrived.

Saturday 24th September – Two-day cricket at Nakuru. Sat with the Mayers. Children stay with the Websters. P insists I make arrangements for Roger to be circumcised.

Thursday 17th September – Chris Walton and a whole covey of photographers arrive. (PR for the company.) Keith Webster says Morag and Michael have German measles.

Saturday 1st October – Mike Ardagh stays, brings us a black Labrador puppy. We call him Shot, after P's dog in India. He's lovely!

Sunday 2nd October – Mike, Keith Webster and P go out shooting in the Northern Grazing Area. They bag 30 kangas [guinea fowl].

Sunday 8th October – Roger is circumcised by Sr. Louisalba. Funny thing for a nun to do. She said she copied the way the Embu tribes do it. I never really understood what she did, never dared to look! We eat our sandwiches with the Cooks.

Sunday 16th October – The new District Officer at Maua, and his wife, come to stay. Andy and Helen Brooks. He's tanned, average height, with incredibly dark blue eyes and long lashes. She is ten years older than him, plain, an ex-nursing sister, they met when he was in hospital. They have no children. We get on well, but she's rather quiet. We're joined by the Websters, Cooks, Mike Ardagh, Evans and Simpson. We eat a curry made by Mr Patel. The men go off shooting. Very enjoyable day, only marred by young Bill burning himself on the smouldering couch grass near the (new) house. All stay for dinner.

Thursday 20th October – P Wright was expected but doesn't turn up. The new ayah burns herself on the couch grass.

Saturday 22nd October – PW arrives and is whisked off to go shooting after tea. Stays the night. Larry Wateridge comes up for the day.

Wednesday 26th October – The Brooks bring the Webster children over to play, kindly send their housegirl to act as ayah.

Wednesday 16th November – We go over in the Land Rover to stay with the Brooks. Pelting rain. The Maua road is a river! We get stuck on the edge of a precipice, ayah, me and three children. Peter leaves us and walks to Maua, followed all the way by a leopard. He would turn and shine his torch in its face. After he arrived there, Andy send a driver to tow us out. Nerve wracking night!

Thursday 17th November – Andy goes into Meru. P returns to the estate. Helen and I sit talking for hours.

Friday 18th November – I see Dr Ware. Coffee with Alicia. Andy returns in the evening. Carruthers is with him, his house has been cut in two by a falling tree.

Saturday 19th November – Coffee with the Wares [he was a Methodist pastor]. We take two Land Rovers down to the Kinna River. I sit next to Andy, he drives. I look at his bare brown thighs and ache with longing. Lovely jaunt, Carruthers and Bob and Ted from Nyeri. In the evening there's a party at the Brooks', we play charades. Great success. Andy and I are in the dining room looking for more glasses. We kiss. We are irresistibly attracted to each other.

Sunday 20th November – Lazy morning. We all drive up to Maua Hill (known as P.C.'s hill after the time we took the Provincial Commissioner up there.) Admire the vast view over most of Kenya in all directions, Serengeti plains, Mountains of the Moon, desert to the north … Play scrabble with the Brooks, everyone else has gone.

Monday 21st November – P leaves early. I go later, with Kamaja the driver and the plants.

Saturday 26th November – Caledonian Dinner. A piper and all the trimmings. Every time they ask him to play another tune he's offered a wee dram of whisky in a quaich (a small shallow saucer-like bowl), consequently the laddie is verra drunk at the end!

Saturday 24th December – Celebrate Xmas today, as we'll be out tomorrow. Otto doesn't come, but Clark Simpson does.

Monday 26th December – Spend the day with the Cooks. Informal dance in the evening at the P and W.

Drought – 1960

The distant dust trail of one man
Appears like many cattle.
Seized by the wind now,
Pelting him with stinging shafts
Films the hopeful eyes that yet
Seek cloud.
Rounded bellies of children
Starvation's little joke
Where are the bright green shoots
Opening out like prayers?
Eddying up, proud-tasselled cobs
Now empty.
Livid and lightning-coloured
Strips of liana bleed in dust
Up the bank, overhead wind
Mauls trees, tearing off twigs
To rain on the parched earth
Bitter rain.
He chews the sustaining stem
Miraa lulling his hunger,
Brushes now by low branches
Treads light on leaf-hidden slime
Stiffly across splashed stones
Of a stream.
Clamouring birdsong, monkey screams
Sibilant plantains, mottled ferns,
The lively fertile buzz all mock,
His drawn cheeks and withered crops.
Brief mirage.

1961

Sunday 8th January – Go fishing on Uaso Nyiro. Camel abattoir on the way. We see a totally naked Turkana run out of a hut with a small 'saucepan' radio, doing a frenetic version of the 'twist'! I suppose he wanted to show us how civilised he was. On the riverbank we spot a small man with a huge barbel over one shoulder. Its head is much bigger than his! The tail drags two feet on the ground behind him ... he keeps tripping over the long whiskers! The fish feed on the camel entrails from the abattoir, which explains the enormous size. It probably feeds a whole village. We go along the river and find a nice shady place, the sun is very hot. I catch a smallish barbel and put it on the river bank beside me, then carry on fishing. I hear a strange squeaking, like a baby crying. It's the fish! I throw it back in, no more fishing for me. Andy and his wife are with us, and some other people from Meru.

Wednesday 11th January – Chris Walton, his wife and mother, plus Jake Kruger, stay one night. They go down to Liliaba to shoot, but only bag one yellow-necked spurfowl.

Saturday 14th January – Cricket at Nyeri. P makes 72 runs. Stay with the Kings. Dinner party with Pam and Gerry Johnston-Hill. Helen, David Ettock and I go back to the cricket club, for the odd dance and much beery singing.

Monday 16th January – Drive back, with punctures all the way. Feed the smalls at the P and W.

Tuesday 17th January – Geoffrey Nye, Erle Green, Ken R, and the D.C. Hodge visit the estate and have coffee with us. Diphtheria injections due.

Monday 30th January – Go to Nairobi. Have all four wisdom teeth out. Agonising pain, mouth distorted, swollen and bloody.

Tuesday 31st January – The Bensolls bring me home to Meru. Angus Hutton is coming up to camp with us.

Saturday 4th February – Cricket at Nyeri. P goes alone, my teeth still aching so I stay at home.

Sunday 5th February – Paint in oils all day. We planned this closed-in glass verandah, which has my easel and paints laid out so I can leave my work and not have to tidy it away every day. I'm painting Mt. Kenya in the background, the foreground has a profusion of indigenous wild flowers, rather ambitious for me, as I'm used to watercolours. But worth a try, so we have a memento of this glorious place.

Monday 6th February – P arrives 2.30 pm. Chief Commissioner due 3.00 pm! Fortunately they're late. Provincial Commissioner, D.C., Burgwin and Andy, Glen Graham and Ashman, the entomologists.

Saturday 11th February – The Hodges to tea, she's back from the UK. The Forses and her brother arrive, stay the night.

Sunday 26th February – Long walkabout to look for the perfect house site for the assistant's house. The Ambler-Davises arrive for lunch. P and Cliff go shooting, bag nine Kangas.

Tuesday 28th February – P goes into Meru. Arrives back very late, the beast! Heard the election results at the club, Jackson and Matè are in (Meru District Council).

Saturday 4th March – Cricket at Nyeri. I leave Roger with the Cooks. Jane and Michael come with us.

Saturday 11th March – Shooting party: Ambler-Davises, Simons, Clark, Websters, Ibbotson, Andy, John Hannoth. Bag 40 birds. Give some to the Mission at Kianjai.

Tuesday 14th March – Play reading at the P and W. Ghastly lack of talent! Robin Lavers, Greaves and us have an illegal fry-up in the kitchen.

Sunday 19th March – Farewell lunch for Websters and Middlebos at Andy's. Awful curry! Andy said he put condensed milk in it, was thinking of coconut milk, perhaps. Cooks are there as well. We all play tennis.

Monday 20th March – Robin King breezes up uninvited, stays the night. We are the local hotel! He stays another night.

Wednesday 22nd March – Anniversary of our arrival here.

Sunday 26th March – The Jouberts come over, have lunch and go for a shoot. P and Shot walk into a pride of lions, two adults and four cubs. He and Shot freeze as the lions amble past ... they must have just eaten. [Or they could have been Elsa and her family, as they were not far from the Adamsons' territory?]

Friday 31st March – Good Friday. Tea with the Hodges. Helen Brooks is there, and the McEntees.

Saturday 1st April – Bake my first loaf of bread, at midnight!

Sunday 2nd April – Watch the East African Safari. Play a little tennis at the Police Club. See an awful film at P and W.

Tuesday 4th April – Sort out our account with Mrs Patel. We're always in the red! [Was it then that I had a curry-making lesson? In a pressure cooker on a primus stove squatting on her kitchen floor.] Tea with Mrs Ambler-Davis. The April rains start.

Saturday 15th April – Roger's last polio injection. See Matè and the Hattersleys. They will be coming to lunch on Saturday if the roads are passable.

Wednesday 10th May – Daddy died. God Rest His Soul (he was only 59).

[I only received Mummy's letter on the 15th. Too late to go to the funeral, even if we could have afforded it. It was Mummy's birthday, and Daddy went out to buy a bottle of wine to celebrate. Didn't come back for hours, but she didn't worry, because he was always going off and getting drunk. This time he was just at the top of the steps leading to their basement flat, but she never even looked out of the door. A couple of youngsters passing by found him next morning. He'd had a massive haemorrhage, but he was still barely alive. An ambulance took him to hospital, where he suffered another haemorrhage and died. Cirrhosis of the liver, caused by years of abuse with whisky. I can't pretend to have loved him, to me he was an ogre, and he made my mother's life a misery, but I feel sorry for him, because they were so mismatched, and she nagged him terribly. He was a good provider, we always had clothes and food and a nice house, and I went to boarding schools and RADA, so he wasn't so bad.]

Monday 15th May – Winduses and Mary Thompson to stay. I receive M's letter. Life has to go on. They stay till Thursday. Wise, Backs and Waltons to lunch.

Monday 29th May – Robin King calls, his baby was born dead. P goes to Nanyuki.

Monday 19th June – Three police officers come for a bath and stay to supper. [They were camped near the estate, looking for the Mau Mau, who lived in the forest around us.]

Thursday 22nd June – Travel to Nakuru. Meet the Winduses at 4.30. Go on to Eldoret.

Wednesday 28th June – Meet Midge Taylor at Nandi Bears Club. Great to see everyone again.

Sunday 2nd July – Travel back to Nandi. Church in the morning.

Thursday 3rd August – Roger's first birthday (and Nan's birthday).

Saturday 12th August – Cricket at Nyeri. Stay with Bob Green. P goes to Nairobi to play squash, Bob takes me to the White Rhino to play skittles – fun!

Saturday 2nd September – Go to Nanyuki Show. [I'm not sure if that was the time the Queen Mum visited Kenya ... anyway she looked lovely in sweet pea colours, my snap of her is partly behind a horse's tail.] Dance at the club in the evening. I see *Fresh Fields*, well acted by the local drama group, 'The Equatorians'. P and I have a row, he goes off to Mawingo. Stay with Ray Letcher. Very cold, only one blanket each.

[We used to have horrible rows in the car on the way home – the children were always so frightened, especially when he made me get out of the car and walk in the dark on the dangerous roads, with Mau Mau lurking about. Thank God for the children, they would scream for him to let me back in the car and eventually he would relent. Usually he was mad drunk, driving all over the road ... I was so unhappy sometimes in those years, I would wander round the perimeter of the estate, hoping the MauMau would capture me and finish me off. Once I started walking down the road leading out of the estate, with the full intention of going all the way to Meru, but he tracked me down in the Land Rover and forced me to get in. He was only worried about what people would think ... after all, he still needed a hostess for all the company events.]

Saturday 16th September – P leaves me at the Heinssens'. Goes on to Nairobi. I see *Kim*, with the Cooks. He makes 87 not out against Parklands 2nd XI.

Monday 18th September – He collects the new car, Mercedes diesel, goes to Nandi, interviews Duncan Fleming, our new assistant.

Sunday 24th September – Go to Timau to visit the Murrays [polo-playing, rich-as-Croesus farmers]. They're away so we go to Isiolo instead. P plays golf at Meru Club. Jane drops a clanger to Wendy Harbottle.

Friday 29th September – Go to Nanyuki to see Mrs Laundy re school. Dinner with the Murrays on the way back.

Thursday 5th October – Cricket Festival at Nairobi. Leave Roger and Michael at the Cooks'. Jane goes off to stay with the Jouberts. We go to the Wanderers Club. See Ted Seed and Mark Foster from Kampala. P plays for Central Province. Ted asks us to spend Xmas or New Year with him.

Saturday 7th October – Dance at Parklands. See Brian Purvis – he and Anne are separated. They have four children, it's terrible!

Sunday 8th October – We go to a formal dinner at the club. I choke on a piece of underdone steak. Rush off to the Ladies, but can't cough it up. Back to the dinner table with blood running out of nose and mouth. At last P notices and takes it seriously. Go to Emergency at the hospital. Am only able to breathe a little with my mouth open. The Sikh doctor saves my life. He gets a cotton hanky and holds my tongue forward with it, makes me take short pants and coughs, and at last it comes out – it was lodged between windpipe and oesophagus. It probably happened because I was in an extremely nervous, tense state, that's what living with P did to me. When I thought I was going to choke to death, I wrote him a note – 'for the record, I love you'…

Tuesday 10th October – Lunch with the Donnellys. Robin King stays with us. The Jouberts bring Jane back.

Saturday 14th October – Donnellys and Clark Simpson invited for a shoot. Tons of rain, roads very bad. Only the Heinssens get through, and Clark; he has to stay the night.

Sunday 22nd October – Roads very bad. P goes into Meru, stays with the Heinssens. Waits at the airstrip for the directors for ages.

Monday 23rd October – Wise, Penwill, Rendell, Wallis … plane can barely lift off the airstrip because of the mud. Only Jackson 'Ngaine and his wife come up by car, it causes bad feeling.

Sunday 19th November – The DC and a convoy bring supplies to Kianjai [we were completely marooned]. Roads are still impassable.

Monday 20th November – The Murrays fly over in their Cessna, and drop a package containing two loaves of bread and sweets for the children! Children very excited to see the plane.

Thursday 23rd November – Jane and Michael's birthday, they were very disappointed no children could come to their party, they see so few children as it is.

The next few months I made no entries in my diary. I think the events (re Andy and me), were too traumatic, and I was afraid P would read it, which of course he did later.

We went to Buffalo Springs a few times. This was a bomb crater made by our troops in the Second World War. Beautiful pure water, you could see every pebble, the only disadvantage was the leeches, but the children enjoyed going there, in our new diesel Mercedes, or going to Isiolo in the Northern Grazing Area, where there was a proper swimming pool. They used to have sand yacht and camel races there. Occasionally we'd drop in to see the Adamsons and their lioness, Elsa. Joy had quite a reputation as a nympho. She used to go out and about topless when doing sketches of the tribesmen, which was certainly not done in those days, the local chiefs were disgusted, especially as she had breasts 'like razor strops' (to quote P). She was very Germanic, bossy, but George was nice.

The children needed schooling, so I started on the Rift Valley Correspondence Course. English and art were fine, we all enjoyed those lessons, but arithmetic was hopeless. Jane and Michael would hide among the passion fruit vines on the roof of the servants' quarters, and I called and called and could never find them. I often had to send off their lessons half done, or not at all, I refused to fake their work. The teachers would not accept this situation, so then Jane had to go away to school in Nanyuki or Nyeri, as a weekly boarder. We had to go to Nairobi to buy her uniform.

On one trip to Nairobi we went to a casino. P was gambling and I lost interest. At about 3 o'clock in the morning I found three little gilt chairs, arranged them in a row, and lay down to sleep, flat on my back. P says he eventually came to collect me and found me lying asleep with my eyes wide open, he thought I was dead. I remember I wore a short-skirted silver lamé two-piece, and flat silver shoes. Perhaps I remember it because it was difficult to arrange the skirt to cover my undies when I lay down.

Once our new house was built, and the tea factory almost completed, the Sikh builders suggested we try a TV. Everyone said it was impossible because the Aberdare Mountains were in the way of the signal. Amazingly we received a very good signal, the Sikhs said it must have bounced off the mountains, hit Mount Kenya, and ricocheted back onto us! Whatever the reason, it made a big difference to our isolated life. No one else around us had TV. Admittedly the programmes were pretty limited: re-runs of American sitcoms, or old films (*Bonanza, I Love Lucy, Phil Silvers*). But we did get the news. There was no daytime viewing, only in the evening for a few hours.

Towards the end of 1961 Andy and I had become desperate. We were continuously thrown together. We tried hard to forget the overwhelming attraction, after all we had exchanged only one hurried kiss, but it was no use. He saw how P treated me, as a barely useful chattel, and it hurt him to see this, when he loved me so much. He drove up to the house one day, and we had a talk (before P turned up, having seen his Land Rover pass the factory). The temptation to hold him was agonising, but I stayed at one end of the sitting room and wouldn't let him come near me. I told Andy I couldn't desert the children, but I couldn't bear to see him so often and not be able to show my feelings. I liked Helen very much, I didn't want to hurt her either, but they had married for companionship only, there was no chance of children, and he was much younger than her. I told him I wanted to ask P to avoid seeing them, but Andy said it would cause an impossible situation, as the two of them had to work together over labour-related problems, and the social side was part of it.

On New Year's Eve, at a dance at the club, after a few drinks, I managed to persuade Andy that we must tell P. We went up to him, hand in hand, like a couple of naughty children, I was so naïve. I thought he would understand that we were trying to do the right thing – so many couples had affairs under their partner's noses, but we were honest. I said we were in love, but didn't want to break up our marriages, so for our children's sake the best thing was if we no longer had anything to do with each other socially, that we could make up a story that there had been a row of some sort.

All hell broke loose – I should have sensed what a vicious man P was. He accused us of sleeping together, and nothing we said could convince him otherwise. *He judged us by his own immoral behaviour in India.* He went straight to Donald Hodge the DC, and had Andy sacked from his position at Maua. He talked about it to his drinking chums, so that the story spread all over Meru. Andy was moved to another district, and his name was mud. I heard the squash players sniggering about him, saying he 'sweated like a pig', and he was a 'wog' (he had dark skin), and the wives would stop talking when I came into a room. That was when the iron entered my heart. I had no more respect or affection left for this wicked man. I wished I *had* slept with Andy.

Before the Andy affair came to a head we were under considerable stress from the knowledge that we were on the Mau Mau hit list, as we were so isolated and near the forest. A police spy at one of their meetings had reported that they were planning to kill us. The DC appointed two askaris to patrol round the estate and to guard our house at night. P started to give me shooting lessons with his heavy Luger. The recoil was so great I couldn't control it. He told me to aim at a big tree in the garden, but I missed it each time. The Mau Mau should have felt quite heartened by my display.

On the bad days, after a particularly bitter row with P, I would wander round the edge of the estate, see the remains of the terrorists' bivouacs, little stamped-out fires in odd places, and long for them to finish me off. Once I lay down in the long grass and prayed to God to kill me, a bolt of lightning, anything. Nothing happened, of course, and I felt a bit silly.

Our Labrador, Shot, flushed out a leopard near the labour lines. The headman swore it had unusual markings, very blurred. We looked in our animal book, and the only one similar to his description was the clouded leopard found only in the foothills of the Himalayas!

Our leopard had been the terror of the locals since before we arrived, picking off goats, dogs and sometimes children. Our little smooth-haired terrior, Patch, had bravely had a go, and been badly mauled. We tried various traps, baited by sheep or goats, but the animal was very clever, and could smell humans.

After the New Year, with all the furore about Andy, it seemed a good time for me to go back home. P and I now decided on a trial separation. I would go on ahead, and he would join us later. I was to try to find a job, probably in Broadstone, Dorset, where Nan and Colin were now living. What a trip! Bumpy thermals, Roger wouldn't stop crying, Michael found the Disprin in my bag, and ate two or three, Jane was very restless. Mummy met us at Heathrow, it was very foggy. A doctor treated Michael for the overdose; the children were unused to cold weather; we all got sick; I got bronchitis.

Building The tea factory

1962

Saturday 20th January – Arrive in Dorset by hired car. Staying with Nan and Colin. It's very cold.

Tuesday 23rd January – Jane and Michael start at Springdale Oaks School. We are staying with some neighbours, the Soffes, with two children of their own. Nan and Colin give a little cocktail party to introduce me to their friends.

Tuesday 30th January – We view the house we're going to rent, sharing with Mummy. It'll mean lighting up a coal range every morning, to heat the water – ugh! At the Soffes' I'd hang out Roger's nappies to dry and they would freeze solid. My bronchitis is worse.

Wednesday 31st January – Pay Miss Courtney £1.15s for children's schooling. Letter from P: Patch has faced the leopard in his lair, been mauled again. It's a huge hollow tree, with several rooms, one for eating, one for sleeping, and one for storing food – very clean. The headman has formed a special posse and caught it, it's not a clouded leopard, just an ordinary one, but much bigger than usual.

Saturday 3rd February – Drinks with Nan and Colin and the Dewars, Kyles, Byes. Very pleasant.

Monday 5th February – Pay the Soffes' rent – £7.8s 3d.

Saturday 10th February – See film, *Seagulls over Sorrento*, amusing, with Ronald Shiner.

Friday 2nd March – I buy an oil heater – £5.19s.

Sunday 4th March – Nan and Colin fly overseas [to West Africa, I think].

Monday 5th March – Half term. I move into the house.

Tuesday 6th March – Mummy arrives from London with her baggage, furniture coming tomorrow.

Monday 19th March – Colin flew to Nairobi.

Sunday 3rd June – P on leave. Catch 7.20 fast train to London. Meet him at airport. He's looking well. We stay the night with Pat. Visit the Wig and Pen for drinks, then the Antelope, our old pub, and the George IV.

Friday 29th June – Dance at the Mess. [Were Nan and Colin back?]

Wednesday 1st August – Fanny's birthday. [Later preferred to be called 'Fran'.] Pat and the children come to stay.

Friday 3rd August – Roger's and Nan's birthday. He's two years old. Pat leaves her precious Helena Rubinstein pure silk powder on the dressing table, he spills it all over the carpet – she's absolutely furious!

Monday 6th August – Kongoni cricket tour. P is playing of course. They go all over Devon and Dorset, playing on village greens, with W.G. Grace lookalikes swinging sixes over the steeples! I go to some of them.

Monday 29th August – Tour ends, P is back. We decide the separation doesn't work, can't afford it. I am sick with colds and flu all the time, can't get work. Mummy is driving me mad, she spoils the children and forces them to side with her against me.

Sunday 9th September – Drive down to Wales to stay with P's parents. Stay at the farm at Llandovery. Beautiful countryside. Meet P's brother Richard's two sons, Martin and Adrian.

Wednesday 12th September – Leave for London. Stay at Princess Lodge, Prince of Wales Tce, Kensington. Pleasant hotel.

Thursday 13th September – Dine out with Oscar Mason and his wife. (He's an ex Nandi Hills tea planter, and is on the cricket tour.)

Sunday 16th September – Arrive in Nairobi. Bob Mackay not there to meet us, so we travel on up.

Monday 17th September – Stay the night at the Nanyuki club.

Sunday 29th September – Duncan Cape and Peter Scott (assistants) arrive. We collect Jane from the Cooks. I see the Dr at Meru re Jane's bedwetting. Poor soul, there's so much upheaval in her life.

Thursday 4th October – Fathers Botta, Motta and Roberti from Kianjai to dine. They bring their operatic records. We collect Jane from Nyeri school.

Saturday 6th October – Chris brings Jane over, he goes back with her on Sunday.

Wednesday 10th October – Lord Howick visits the estate. He's on a fact-finding tour from the UK.

Here the diary ends abruptly – it must have suffered from the inroads of the damp trunk.

I had several driving lessons in the Land Rover, with our driver, but ended ignominiously stuck in a ploughed field with a flooded engine. My studio was my refuge. I painted an imaginary portrait of a torso of an African man. He had a yellow cloth over one shoulder, turquoise sky behind him. He was a composite of the best attributes of the local tribes, warm brown skin, high cheekbones, proud fierce bearing. Our new African DC saw it and insisted on buying it. I had no idea what to charge, but settled for 5 guineas! It was the first one I had sold.

1963

Andy and his wife were long gone, I had no idea where, but I hoped he was relatively happy. At least he'd got away from Peter. The Mau Mau were becoming very brash now, they smelled uhuru (freedom) coming, and started venturing out of their forest hideouts. Smelling vile, with filthy dreadlocks and wearing rags or animal skins, they were a terrifying sight. We had heard that most of them had been forced to take oaths that violated all their tribal taboos, under threats to their families, so they had become outcasts. Jomo Kenyatta, the civilised, educated, London School of Economics graduate, had dreamed up these satanic oaths. I could sympathise with their desire for independence, but the barbarous methods they used, which included ham-stringing cattle, and luring the very whites who had succoured their tribe to horrible deaths – that was inexcusable.

In November, one night at about 11 pm, I was watching the news, and a flash came up: President Kennedy had been shot in Dallas. He was one of my idols, the young, handsome, idealistic leader … at the time hardly anyone outside the States had any idea that he was possibly bankrolled by the Mafia, and a sexual predator. We thought he was the hope of the Western world! I cried bitterly, it was like losing a close relative. A priest came up from Kianjai, Father Ferguson, a Scots Catholic. I started a course of instruction with him, I felt I badly needed to find a faith to help me endure and to carry on with the dismal life with P.

Mr Patel, the duka owner who was our friend, was robbed of his goods and a truck by the Mau Mau. Apparently this was a normal procedure, they just went into any shop and took what they wanted without paying.

Jane was going to have to go to school with strapping 12-year-old African boys sitting in the same class, (she was just 8), I was worried about what could happen to her.

For some time now P had been smuggling tea seed and plants through to our parent company, Sapekoe, in South Africa, via places like Angola and Swaziland. The Kenya government had boycotted SA because of the apartheid policies, and no one was allowed to send anything there, officially.

Peter Wright, our Director, came to stay with us, without his wife. One evening, when P was still out on the estate, he began to tell me that P was not doing his work satisfactorily, and was due to be sacked for inefficiency. P's vile temper was not helped by the awful hangovers from drinking with the cronies at the Meru Club, or the Pig and Whistle, and this did not cement good labour relations. Peter W. knew about Fergus's death, Andy, and our trial separation, so he was onto an easy situation, playing on my resentment. He hinted that if I was 'nice' to him, P could retain his job.

I was incredibly frustrated, and Peter was a very attractive man. He started kissing me, which led to petting, then P walked in. We leaped apart, but he said nothing, pretended everything was normal. The next day P went out to work early (for a change) and PW called me into his room and asked for tea. When I brought it to him he started trying to seduce me again, but I was disgusted and told him so.

After he left P hauled me over the coals, and refused to believe that PW had threatened the sack, it was one more stick to beat me with. Strangely enough his attitude to work improved considerably after that...

Somali Girl

1964

Sunday 5th January – Jane goes back to school. Have heard we are definitely leaving Kenya. I wish we could go back to UK.

Sunday 26th January – Outing for Jane. We go swimming at the Outspan Hotel, all very sunburnt.

Tuesday 28th January – Chief Samson comes to say goodbye. I finish my oil painting of Mt Kenya, with local wildflowers in the foreground.

Saturday 1st February – We leave the estate. Go to 'Nkubu, then lunch at the P and W. Drinking companions Paddy Johnson, Brian Edmondson, Simeon Kimande. We dance. I meet a woman who tells me the polite phrase in South Africa is 'Jou praat kak'! Later in SA I repeat this, to everyone's delighted horror (it means you're talking shit!). We dance a conga, to Trini Lopez's song 'Yellow Bird'. Simeon's hands on my hips curiously exciting.

Tuesday 4th February – Dinner with the Patels. Their curry not as good as of yore. Various civic dignitaries there as well. Children are with the Simons.

Wednesday 5th February – Dinner with Brian Edmondson. Father Ferguson comes. Gives me a book *All you Ever Wanted to Know about Roman Catholicism*. Questions and answers, some unintentionally funny.

Friday 7th February – Tea with Father Eandi at Engadeni. Beautiful country, bracken, red soil, just like Nyambeni. Pecuana tree with drooping clusters of brown flowers. Michael rides on the mare Tosca, who is in foal. It reminds me of the time I went riding when five months pregnant with Roger, that mare was also in foal. [We had visited the Bevans. Their children had mumps, and Peter Bevan was afraid he would catch it and become impotent.] My horse was just grazing on a loose rein while I looked at the view, when something spooked her, maybe a snake, but whatever it was, she took off for home like a bolt of lightning. I hung on, but my tummy rather got in the way. Halfway up a hill leading to their stable, I noticed a tree with an overhanging branch. I just managed to bend low enough to scrape under it, otherwise I should either have been scalped or beheaded. We heard she'd died of a stroke three days later. I was a bit nervous of horses after that.

Thursday 13th February – Half term, we collect Jane. Carry on to Nairobi. Next day on to Mtito Andei. Very tiring trip. The tarmac road stretches further than we had expected, but then it's dusty murrum full of pot holes. The children wake up, so we carry on a few hours more. Meet up with Harry Tunmer from Nandi, with his mother.

Friday 14th February – Sleep beside the road. Watch a marvellous dawn, cool and crisp, with the tangy smell of dust and khaki bush. Breakfast at the Manor House Hotel in Mombasa. We visit the Sutherlands. Very hot and noisy at night, it's the Muslim festival – Id-Ul-Fitr. See *Hero's Island* with James Mason.

Sunday 16th February – Board the *Braemar Castle*. B Deck, very hot. First sitting at meals. Food is superb. The waiter has a Beatle haircut! Lovegrove sees off Bernard Smith and his family. There is a strike in Dar-Es-Salaam, so we can't land for water and supplies, go on to Beira, same thing. There is no fresh water. The pool is empty. All we can drink is bottled or canned drinks. Roger comes out in big spots. Ship's doctor diagnoses chickenpox. Turning into a truly horrible trip, we feel so hot and dirty.

Monday 24th February – Arrive in Durban. Big bustling port. Reporters interview us and our picture is in the local paper! I'm just so glad to have a bath. We are staying at the Federal Hotel in West Street (at the expense of the government for three months). Very noisy verandah room. Traffic all night, but at least it's near the sea. Our ears are unused to the bustle.

1964

Arrived From East Africa

FEB 24ª 1964

MR. PETER BLANDY and his wife, Sheila, and their children (from left) Michael (5), Roger (3) and Jane (8), who were among the immigrants from East Africa who arrived aboard the Braemar Castle in Durban yesterday. Mr. Blandy, an Oxford rugby Blue who captained Uganda against the touring Rhodes University team in 1956, was a tea planter in the Meru district, Kenya. "With several hundred long-haired gents coming out of the forests, it was getting a bit hot for us there," he said.

Our arrival is reported in the local paper

Our last family photo in Kenya

169

Jane at Nelspruit Show

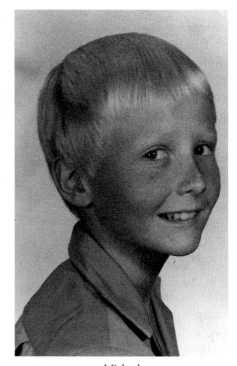

Michael

Roger

Tuesday 25th February – Roger has been kept in a darkened room as per the ship's doctor's instructions, but he isn't getting better, his spots have turned into large blisters all over his body. We take him to Addington Hospital. He has a streptococcal infection, probably caused by a mosquito bite in Mombasa, and the unhygienic conditions on board the ship caused the infection to run riot. They give me an ointment, we have to prick each blister and rub it in. He is so brave, doesn't cry or whimper but endures it with a smile.

Sunday 1st March – I go to St Peter's Church. Talk to the young priest afterwards. We go swimming on the beach with the Smiths, P looks after Roger.

Monday 2nd March – Walking with the children in West St. They are not used to heavy traffic, and run around in all directions ... I have to have eyes in the back of my head. I bark my shin on the sharp end of a slatted seat placed alongside the kerb. [The resultant bruise never goes away, ends up as a varicose vein.] Sheila Smith and I go to the aquarium in the evening. Meet a pleasant Rhodesian woman there. P and Bernard Smith only come back in the early hours of the morning.

Tuesday 3rd March – Bus trip around Durban, looked at the dry docks, huge, fascinating. Tea at the golf course. There are monkeys there. P and Bernard go to Johannesburg.

Tuesday 10th March – The children are now going to the school in Point Road. It's a bad area, but at least it's near to the hotel. P comes back, he's been to see Gamble, Phil de Wet.

Thursday 11th March – I meet David Dunlop, Ham Hamilton, they are connected with entertainment in Durban. Take us to meet Cindy Ryder, a singer, and Al Ewing, who has a band. They live on a kind of barge beside the Esplanade.

Monday 16th March – Possible job for me at the *Daily News*.

Wednesday 18th March – Commercial radio audition with Yolande

D'Hotman at Scotswood Buildings. To my amazement my old voice production teacher from RADA is there, Miss King! She looks exactly the same, black hair scraped back in a bun, severe black suit – great to see her again! We go to watch Peter Snell run the mile at King's Park, 3 mins. 59.7 seconds, very good.

Thursday 19th March – Give Miss Schoeman a deposit of 2 guineas for a six-week modelling course.

Saturday 21st March – First session of Charm School.

Tuesday 24th March – Audition with June Davidson at 18 Muthaiga Place. We have tea, read the play, *A Hatful of Rain* by Clifford Odets. All about drug pushers in America.

Tuesday 31st March – Radio audition, bring own script.

Tuesday 7th April – Instruction with Father Holland. Start working for H.F. Goddard, selling office equipment, dymo tape – cold canvassing. A schlep!

Thursday 16th April – Audition SABC, Humphry Gilbert. Do various dialects.

Friday 17th April – Meet Robin Alexander at Alma and Howell Cobbledick's (radio producer). Am on the SABC casting list now.

Saturday 25th April – Last lesson at Charm School. They taught me umbrella twirling and managing gloves, already totally out of date, but SA were always a year behind.

Monday 27th April – Radio with Yo D'Hotman.

Thursday 7th May – P takes us to Ifafa on the south coast. It's a lagoon, and the river is low. We waterski – I hang on like mad, but can't seem to rise onto the skis, instead plough along under the surface! P's thinking of buying it and turning it into a resort. We have no money, surely the bank won't lend us any?

Saturday 12th May – Get a list of photographers from Desia at the Charm School. We've moved to the Casa Mia hotel, a real dump, but the govt. have stopped paying for us. Horrible landlady.

Thursday 14th May – Take Michael to Addington hospital for an x-ray. [Chest?]

Monday 18th May – Audition with Anne Freed for radio work at Shelton Bldngs.

Wednesday 3rd June – Robert Gorneman, Geray studios. Taken particulars. Collect script at SABC. Photos with Ian McLunan.

Friday 5th June – Appt. with Virginia Lee, she might be my singing teacher. She's a brassy blonde, and her ideas are completely wrong, wants me to sing *eeees* with a tight throat and stretched mouth, can't learn with her.

Saturday 6th June – Someone recommended Ali Arletovich as a singing teacher. He's sweet. Pudgy, fair curly hair, receding hairline. He has a curly mouth too, used to smiling! He encourages me, so I sing much better. The only problem is, he's a toucher, likes to stroke my thigh, accidentally on purpose as he passes.

Mr Hardman tells me my typing isn't good enough, so I'm out of work again. Ring Humphry Gilbert for radio work. I try to sell office equipment, but no one wants to buy it. I meet Micho, who sits swinging his leg violently as I give him my sales pitch – I'm so naïve I don't realise what he's doing!

Saturday 13th June – P leaves for Tzaneen.

Tuesday 16th June – See *The Happiest Days of Your Life*, very funny. Meet Peter Craig and Barry Welman, who introduce me to Des Morley, who arranges concerts of singing and dancing.

Around this time I go out for a drink with Micho, and I meet Clifford Hooker. He is a pleasant easy-going chap, a rugby player, in his mid thirties, with dark curly hair and warm brown eyes. He shows me the tenderness I had been missing for years. We start an affair. Subconsciously I was looking for someone to replace P, someone who would be kind to my children. By the time I got to know Clifford really well, and realised that he was an irresponsible person, a lightweight, I was pregnant. For years I had had no reason to use any birth control, had stopped the pill so, of course, I was extremely fertile.

Wednesday 24th June – Recording at SABC 5.45.

Saturday 27th June – Cocktail party at university, Chepstone Hall. Meet Professor Elizabeth Sneddon, an indomitable person – so vibrant!

Wednesday 1st July – Move to Phoenix Hotel in West St, slight improvement on Casa Mia.

Thursday 2nd July – Interview with David Horner of Napac (Natal Performing Arts). June D. says bookings are good for the play, so it's on again. Must study a coloured accent for a radio play.

Monday 6th July – Go to Chamber of Commerce re a job. Meet Prof. Sneddon with a view to job at uni.

Wednesday 8th July – Singing with Ali.

Friday 10th and Saturday 11th July – Record radio play.

Wednesday 22nd July – Fourth singing lesson. Ring up Peter Craig re joining Yacht Club.

Thursday 23rd July – Start Method Acting classes with Keith van der Wat. Am given a comp. to the Lyric Theatre.

Wednesday 22nd July – Start rehearsing *Hatful of Rain*.

174

Thursday 30th July – Rehearsal for *Out of the Night*, radio play.

Saturday 1st August – Move into a sordid flat.

Sunday 2nd August – Rehearsal for concert at the City Hall. I'm singing 'Fly me to the Moon', 'Yellow Bird' (Trini Lopez), the Burl Ives 'Cherry' song.

Monday 3rd August – Roger's fourth birthday. Record *Front Page Story* (play) for Yo D'Hotman.

Friday 7th August – Record 'A Stake in the Land', a talent programme for immigrants, I sing the Cherry song unaccompanied.

Saturday 8th August – P and I have a major row. He decides to divorce me. He insists on taking Michael and Jane back to Barberton with him. They are crying, hanging on to me, but he tears them away – it's awful! Thank goodness Roger is still with me.

Sunday 30th August – Publicity photos for the play, Roger is in some of them as well. We go to Cato St. June wants us to look part of the play's drug addict scene, so it's hanging around the back streets. Pauline Segorin gives us a lift home. I have been very sick. Can't stop vomiting.

Wednesday 9th September – Ring Mrs Stewart of the *Natal Mercury* to arrange an interview.

Sunday 13th September – First rehearsal of *Hatful*. I play the druggie, it's a walk-on really.

Friday 18th September – I have a back street abortion. Later, Peter arrives and moves us out of that nasty flat into a lovely room at the Palm Beach Hotel. He needs a housekeeper still.

Saturday 19th September – Takes me out to dinner at a nice restaurant. We decide to try and carry on together – no divorce. I can hardly believe his change of attitude! [Some weeks later I realise that he was only humouring me to get me back into harness, so to speak, the way he humours a sick horse, he's always good with animals.] He has to go back to Barberton, and I have a commitment to do the play.

Thursday 24th September – At Carmen's flat. She's a good friend, we take turns babysitting each other's children. I met her when we were staying at the Federal Hotel. She used to play the organ there in the evening during Happy Hour. She always wore her dark hair in a heavily lacquered pompadour.

Friday 25th September – Lunch with the Ambler-Davises from the P and W in Meru. Ring Mrs Sharp. June Davidson phones, they've cut out my part in the play. I'm glad, it's hard, working all day, looking after Roger, finding a babysitter, and doing the play. She doesn't want to pay the extra salary.

Saturday 26th September – The Sharps take me to see *A Hard Day's Night*. I fall in love with the Beatles!

Monday 28th September – I buy a cheap guitar (R9) from Gallo's, so I can learn to accompany my songs, that's if I can find someone to teach me.

Tuesday 29th September – See *A Hard Day's Night* again! I'm hooked. Des Corrigan and Barry Melson take me to hear Johnny McGregor at the Playhouse, and Johnny Angel at the Playboy restaurant on the beachfront. Great!

Wednesday 30th September – Method Acting class with Keith van der Wat. I'm helping him teach the class.

Thursday 1st October – Go to East African Society with the Sharps. Phone Miss Little re Napac auditions, maybe in January.

Monday 5th October – Singing. Dressmaker. See *Meet Me by Moonlight*, musical play with Julie Wilson – excellent.

Wednesday 7th October – Last singing lesson. Ali knows Val Miller in Joburg. Last Method class.

Saturday 10th October – Collect my Mt. Kenya oil painting from Salisbury Arcade. See *The Miser* (Moliere), at the Jewish Club. Brickhill Burke, very good.

Sunday 11th October – P has come to fetch us, leave for Barberton.

Wednesday 4th November – Great to be back with all my children together again! My Own Tea Estate is really beautiful, we're on the top of a hill with a gorgeous view. Living in a temporary house on the site of the new one.

Saturday 21st November – Jane and Michael's birthday party. The two Jordan children come. Mick Jordan is P's assistant. We are now living in the new house. I'm busy making a garden, with a rockery. The end of the garden is the sheer rocky drop to the valley below, so I just add more rocks to the existing ones. [P had started grilling me every day, trying to find out who had fathered the baby. His kind act fell away as soon as we arrived in Barberton.]

Sunday 22nd November – Cricket at Eland's Valley. The cricketers were a friendly crowd. I used to score sometimes, a great honour! Our hosts were the Shaws, a wealthy couple with horses, played polo, and flew their own plane, like the Murrays of Timau. [Years later they were killed flying that plane.]

No more diary for a long time because I was too unhappy to bother filling it in. So these are my recollections.

Penny Rogers, née Kane-Burman, moved in with her mother and small son, Guy, at a nearby farm. They came to visit us, and P was very struck with her. She flattered him by showing an inordinate interest in how a tea estate was run. He showed her round, of course (while I made small talk with her mother, who was pleasant enough). She thought he had lots of money, and vice versa, complete misconceptions! She had recently been divorced from a Zimbabwean

TV presenter, Pat Rogers, who later came down to SA and made a name for himself. The rumour was that she'd divorced him because he was gay ... still, he remarried to a lovely model, and no one ever mentioned his so-called gay past. P started an affair with her, and made little effort to conceal it. In a way it was a relief, diverted his attention from my crimes.

Another neighbour was Louis Barnes. He was a descendant of the composer Richard Wagner, and had the same ice-blue eyes. He owned a huge tract of pine forest around us. We often visited him. In Barberton the Murrays owned the Impala Hotel, Dan was Scots of course, and she was a dumpy little blonde, both very kind people.

P bought some horses: a crossed Lesotho pony, virtually untrained, a dainty brown mare for Jane to ride, two ex-racehorses, and a mad swivel-eyed roan nag! Jane was a natural, utterly fearless, but Flamingo was quite a handful and I could never understand why P, the expert rider, didn't school the pony himself. We used to go to gymkhanas at Piggs Peak in Swaziland. What a beautiful country, so lush, rolling vistas, forests, and the Swazis were the friendliest people, always smiling. We went to the Nelspruit Show with Flamingo, and Jane rode her in several novice events, she was in her element! She camped out with other young riders, learnt how to feed and groom the ponies, how to curry comb and brush them, how to look after the tack.

P said I should try to ride again (I hadn't done so for years). One morning he saddled up Flamingo for me. Only when I was astride her did I notice he'd put on half stirrups (easier to fall out of) – this didn't exactly give me confidence! Just at the top of our road I saw him driving the white pick-up truck up the hill towards me. Flamingo began to react badly; she hated it, as she'd arrived on the estate in it, and he knew she hated that vehicle. She started rearing up, then raced down the hill, I lost my balance and hung round her neck, then I fell off and tumbled down the steep stony hillside. Flamingo went berserk and galloped off and was only found later, miles away on the edge of the estate, tangled up in the reins. Luckily my injuries were minor, I felt such an idiot. But later I wondered ... was he just trying to show me up, or were there more sinister motives?

The Transvaal Scottish had been given the freedom of the town of Barberton, and visited once a year. So they marched through the streets with pipes and drums, kilts flying. That evening there was a dance, Michael and Roger stayed in the office on the shiny sofas. Roger had been hit by a telephone pole (carried by a rival gang led by Michael) and had a huge bump on his forehead. They couldn't sleep because of the noise. I had been dancing with a handsome boy, a piper called Bill Fourie. We found we had a lot in common, and there was an instant mutual attraction. He came with me to see how the boys were getting on. The sight of this strapping chap in all his regimental glory, bonnet and sporran, inspired the boys, and they begged him to play the pipes. So he brought them back to the dingy office and marched up and down playing laments and marches! P of course was propping up the bar, he never thought to ask me to dance. (This episode started a love of music in both of them, which lasted through the years.) Bill asked if he could write to me, but I explained how vengeful P was, and that if he did write it would have to be poste restante.

One morning Mick Jordan, our assistant, came to introduce us to a good friend of his who was visiting from Ceylon. His name was Peter Ferguson. I shook hands with this rather bloated-looking gent, then I began to realise this was my long lost cousin, Peter! So then we hugged and exchanged some family news, while P and Jordan looked on, somewhat bemused. Pat had prayed for a member of my family to come and help me, and here he was. Needless to say, he didn't know that was his mission, and soon went away again, but oddly enough just seeing him gave me a kind of strength.

Darryl the surveyor, his wife and three daughters were friends of ours, they often visited the estate. Michael and Roger liked the girls. When we went shopping I sometimes left the children with them. P was drinking heavily at the Impala Hotel, arriving home in the small hours, and his work suffered accordingly.

There was trouble in the labour lines. A man claimed to have magic powers, said that to haunt his enemies he could summon up a tokoloshe (a small hairy goblin type of familiar with a very long penis which he was reputed to sling over his shoulder). P called in a witchdoctor to 'sniff out' the malcontent. Eventually he was discovered, his hut searched and he was arrested. That evening there was a terrifying thunderstorm. The witchdoctor called at the house with his bag of tricks. He had a goatskin draped around his shoulders, with the legs hanging down, and he smelled terrible. As we watched he hauled out a marmite jar, a small bottle containing white powder and another dark bottle. These all belonged to the troublemaker. He said the marmite jar contained the tokoloshe … he opened it and closed it quickly. I saw something dark, hairy.

P laughed at him, but I felt a sense of ancient evil in that small array of potions. P said he wanted to keep the 'muti'. The witchdoctor said no, it would cause trouble in our house, he must take the stuff away with him. P said he wanted to take it to a chemist for analysis, offered the dirty old man five rand and a bottle of brandy, which he grudgingly accepted and scuttled out of the house into the storm. P locked it in his desk, then locked the study door. He said no one must go in there. Because the house was new, there was no grass around it. A sandstorm blew up and deposited sand all over the back of the house, and as the study window was slightly open, it piled up on the study floor. I wanted the houseboy to clean it up but P refused to let him go in there.

Some weeks later the door was still locked. During that time I began to have horrifying fancies of poisoning P with the muti. I would be busy planting out seedlings, and these dark thoughts invaded my mind. I thought I was going mad. Finally I realised that I had to get rid of the poisons before my mind was totally unbalanced. I found where P had hidden the key, and the ayah and I took the stuff and put it in a small bag. I told her to take it a long way from the house and bury it. P came home in the evening and said he had received a complimentary letter from our directors. He wanted to show it to me, so he went into the study, saw it had been cleaned up, checked the locked drawer and found the stuff was missing. He went into a tantrum, bullying me until I admitted the ayah had buried it somewhere. It was late at night, but he forced her to go out in the dark with him and dig it up again. Then he put it in the top of our bedroom cupboard. I moved into the children's bedroom, I couldn't bear to be in the same room. The children were away at boarding school, even poor little Roger, who was only four. The next night P was out as usual and I lay trying to sleep, but with the sickening awareness of what was in the next room.

The next day we went into Barberton to do the weekly shopping. Afterwards I went on my own to visit Thelma, Darryl's wife. While she was making coffee, I looked idly around the sitting room. In the bookcase I noticed a large blue book, *The Meaning of Truth* by Ernest Holmes. I don't know what impelled me to pick out this book, but anyhow, I asked her if I could borrow it. That night I sat reading it for hours. P was out, probably with Penny. Now – I can't even tell you what the gist of the book was, but it opened up an immense vista of the universe, our puny planet, and my unimportant life in the overall scheme of things. I stared out at the star-filled sky. A new sense of power over my own future filled me. I started writing fluently with my right hand. I could do anything … no longer in the thrall of Peter Blandy. So now the challenge couldn't be ignored. I had to go to the bedroom cupboard and face up to the reality, break the spell, if you like. I had a brandy to give me Dutch courage. I thought of the words that had inspired me, metaphorically squared my shoulders, and crept along the passage. I was terrified as I opened the cupboard. Something long and furry fell on my face – I remember screaming, then I must have blacked out.

It was dawn when P came home. He found me lying on the floor, my mohair stole wrapped around me. He shook me, dabbed my face with cold water. When I came to, and saw the stole lying on me I found this incredibly funny. Started laughing, couldn't stop! He slapped me, and this goaded me into a fury. I began hitting and kicking him with all my might. Naturally he was much stronger than me, and he grabbed my hands and threw me down. I had nothing to lose. I told him I was leaving as soon as he gave me the money for my train fare.

'What about the children? You can't take them with you.'

'I know, but I have to get away from you. I'm no good to them as I am, I've become so neurotic as a result of your treatment of me, I've been planning to put poison in your food – that muti has invaded my mind. You deliberately put it in the bedroom to drive me mad, and you nearly succeeded. The witchdoctor was right, he said it would cause trouble in this house. Our marriage is a farce, I know you're having an affair with Penny, you should be glad, you'll be free to marry her.'

For once he had nothing to say. Then he rallied, 'You must promise not to fight for custody of the children.'

'I promise.'

'All right, I'll give you money for your fare.'

The witchdoctor

1965

We went to visit the children at half term. It was Roger's fifth birthday. I gave him his presents and hugged him hard. How could I explain to him that I was leaving? One of the many reasons was the fact that P insisted on sending him to boarding school a year before it was necessary, so as to deprive me of my last baby, the baby he refused to believe was his own child. Jane and Michael didn't know I was leaving, and must have wondered why I was crying so much. (I wrote to Jane once I got to Joburg, and tried to explain in understandable terms. I knew that I had to find a lawyer, and would definitely break my promise to P that I wouldn't fight for custody.)

He put me on the train to Johannesburg, with two suitcases, my ticket and 20 rand. Apart from leaving my children behind, I left the pictures I'd painted, clothes, ornaments, a sewing machine, typewriter, and the few friends I'd made. I did return that book to Darryl. He didn't realise what a difference it had made to all our lives.

I had to look for an inexpensive hotel. I found one in the directory that would charge me 20 rand for the two weeks till the end of August. The New Stephanie, in High Street Berea, was hardly new … it had definitely seen better days. The food was barely edible, and they would give me a thin sandwich for lunch. Town was a long walk, with no money for bus fares, but I had to find a job.

I went past a playground, and my longing at the sight of those carefree children was unbearable. My feet developed corns and bunions from walking in unsuitable plastic shoes. On the Monday I went into a department store, Stuttafords, which had a branch in Durban. I'd liked going in there because the staff were polite and didn't hassle the customers to buy. Mrs Davison, the personnel manager, interviewed me. I told her my sad story and she believed me.

The next day I started work as a counter hand, the lowest rung, but I was so happy. At the end of the month I would get 42.50 rand (half salary). I knew I could survive.

Index

Page references in *italic* indicate illustrations.